W9-DJB-060

emotionally intelligent leadership

for Students

Praise for *Emotionally Intelligent Leadership for Students: Student Workbook, Second Edition*

"The student workbook will bring emotionally intelligent leadership to life through a variety of experiential activities, reflective exercises, and a diverse array of resources. A must-have for developing emotionally intelligent leadership!"

—Corey Seemiller, *director, Leadership Programs, University of Arizona*

———————————

"This workbook provides hands-on, intentional teaching and practice of the nineteen capacities of Emotionally Intelligent Leadership. Through active and reflective student learning modules, the workbook presents creative, relevant, and diverse facilitation, application, and assessment strategies."

—Laura Osteen, *director, Center for Leadership and Social Change, Florida State University*

———————————

"The concepts presented here are essential as students become balanced leaders who are driven by responsibility, integrity, and a desire to build relationships among those they serve."

—Leah K. Eickhoff, *program development coordinator, Alpha Sigma Alpha*

———————————

"As we continue to develop the next generation of leaders, we need more resources aimed at helping us understand the 'why' behind our actions, the nuances that make each of us unique and special human beings. This ability to understand others, in addition to ourselves, provides the foundation for everything else we do in leadership development."

—A. Paul Pyrz, Jr., *president, LeaderShape*

second
edition

emotionally
intelligent
leadership
for Students

Student Workbook

**Marcy Levy Shankman,
Scott J. Allen, and
Paige Haber-Curran**

JB JOSSEY-BASS™
A Wiley Brand

Cover design by Wiley

Copyright © 2015 by Marcy Levy Shankman, Scott J. Allen, Paige Haber-Curran. All rights reserved.

Published by Jossey-Bass
A Wiley Brand
One Montgomery Street, Suite 1200, San Francisco, CA 94104-4594—www.wiley.com

No part of this publication may be reproduced, stored in a retrieval system, or transmitted in any form or by any means, electronic, mechanical, photocopying, recording, scanning, or otherwise, except as permitted under Section 107 or 108 of the 1976 United States Copyright Act, without either the prior written permission of the publisher, or authorization through payment of the appropriate per-copy fee to the Copyright Clearance Center, Inc., 222 Rosewood Drive, Danvers, MA 01923, 978-750-8400, fax 978-646-8600, or on the Web at www.copyright.com. Requests to the publisher for permission should be addressed to the Permissions Department, John Wiley & Sons, Inc., 111 River Street, Hoboken, NJ 07030, 201-748-6011, fax 201-748-6008, or online at www.wiley.com/go/permissions.

Limit of Liability/Disclaimer of Warranty: While the publisher and author have used their best efforts in preparing this book, they make no representations or warranties with respect to the accuracy or completeness of the contents of this book and specifically disclaim any implied warranties of merchantability or fitness for a particular purpose. No warranty may be created or extended by sales representatives or written sales materials. The advice and strategies contained herein may not be suitable for your situation. You should consult with a professional where appropriate. Neither the publisher nor author shall be liable for any loss of profit or any other commercial damages, including but not limited to special, incidental, consequential, or other damages. Readers should be aware that Internet Web sites offered as citations and/or sources for further information may have changed or disappeared between the time this was written and when it is read.

Jossey-Bass books and products are available through most bookstores. To contact Jossey-Bass directly call our Customer Care Department within the U.S. at 800-956-7739, outside the U.S. at 317-572-3986, or fax 317-572-4002.

Wiley publishes in a variety of print and electronic formats and by print-on-demand. Some material included with standard print versions of this book may not be included in e-books or in print-on-demand. If this book refers to media such as a CD or DVD that is not included in the version you purchased, you may download this material at http://booksupport.wiley.com. For more information about Wiley products, visit www.wiley.com.

ISBN: 9781118821824 (paperback)

ISBN: 9781118821886 (ebk.)

ISBN: 9781118821879 (ebk.)

Printed in the United States of America

SECOND EDITION

PB Printing 10 9 8 7 6 5 4 3 2 1

CONTENTS

PREFACE

Emotionally intelligent leadership (EIL) is built on the premise that leadership can be developed and learned. The caveat, though, is that leadership development is a process, and it takes a great deal of deliberate practice, reflection, and hard work to truly grow as a leader. The *Emotionally Intelligent Leadership: Student Workbook, Second Edition* serves as a tool to help facilitate your leadership development journey.

About Emotionally Intelligent Leadership

Emotionally intelligent leadership (EIL) promotes an intentional focus on three facets: consciousness of self, consciousness of others, and consciousness of context. Across the three EIL facets are nineteen capacities that equip individuals with the knowledge, skills, perspectives, and attitudes to achieve desired leadership outcomes. The model integrates what we have identified as the best thinking on emotional intelligence and leadership by drawing upon three sources: our own experiences, the experiences of students with whom we have worked, and the larger bodies of literature on emotional intelligence and leadership.

Emotionally Intelligent Leadership: A Guide for Students, Second Edition is the primary EIL text, which includes in-depth information on the model as a whole and chapters addressing each of the EIL facets and capacities. Our hope is that by now you have read *Emotionally Intelligent Leadership: A Guide for Students* or that you will be reading it in conjunction with using this *Student Workbook*.

An overview of the EIL model with definitions of the three facets and nineteen capacities is presented in Appendix A.

About the *Student Workbook*

Emotionally Intelligent Leadership: Student Workbook, Second Edition is a tool that allows you to dig deeper, reflect, and apply the concepts of EIL to your life. Here you will find chapters on each of the EIL facets and capacities. Each chapter contains information about the facet or capacity, additional resources for further learning, quotes from well-respected authorities, and a variety of activities that allow you to explore the concepts in your life, critically engage with the content, reflect upon the material, and apply concepts to case studies.

The *Student Workbook* is designed in conjunction with the *Facilitation and Activity Guide, Second Edition*. Activities referenced in the *Facilitation and Activity Guide* are included here in the *Student Workbook*. Although a majority of the activities included in the *Student Workbook* can be completed on your own, there are some that are directly linked to activities in the *Facilitation and Activity Guide* and will not make sense on their own—we have noted on the activity itself when this is the case.

The *Student Workbook* also complements the *Emotionally Intelligent Leadership for Students: Inventory, Second Edition*. The *Inventory* provides an opportunity to explore experiences in leadership with a focus on identifying strengths and areas for improvement based on past behaviors. The *Inventory* also advances the learning from the present into the future with a focus on self-improvement and leadership development. Based on your results from the *Inventory*, you can tailor your approach to using the *Student Workbook* to best address your leadership development goals.

Developing Emotionally Intelligent Leadership

Developing leadership is a process. The *Student Workbook* is one tool to assist with this journey, but we know it alone is not enough. Of utmost importance is your level of intentionality. Effective leadership takes commitment, awareness, and focused attention. You have to *want* to develop your leadership abilities, and this requires changes in behavior. Effective leadership takes practice—and if you want to improve your knowledge, skills, and abilities, you must take the time and devote your attention to the process.

With intentional practice and focused attention, the facets and capacities of EIL can be learned and developed. However, each requires balance. The trick is recognizing the dynamic nature of leadership—what is needed for a situation will vary based on context. In other words, an appropriate capacity in one situation may be inadequate in another situation. To intentionally engage in leadership development, we recommend first and foremost focusing on three key areas: your relationships, your experiences, and your attitudes.

Relationships: Relationships are an essential part of developing leadership. Whether it is a friend, supervisor, mentor, group member, or family member, a key relationship can be pivotal in helping challenge and support you in your leadership journey. Enlist others in your leadership development journey—let them know the areas in which you are seeking to grow and develop, observe them and ask them questions, ask to work on a project with them, and seek feedback from them to help you grow. Who are the key people in your life who can assist you in your leadership journey? What types of relationships should you seek out?

Experiences: Leadership involves engagement and action. Thus, seek out key experiences that will allow you to engage in and practice the capacities you hope to develop. For some people this may be volunteering at an event, bringing up an alternate point of view in a meeting, or leading a new initiative. We grow through new experiences that take us out of our comfort zone. We call these edge experiences. You know you are at your edge when you have a nervous feeling in your stomach—a feeling of uncertainty as to how things will turn out. Being at the edge requires some risk taking, and through this risk taking there is often much reward and learning. What is your edge? What experiences will take your abilities to a new level? And, who can support and challenge you along the way?

Attitudes: A key component of your development is the attitude with which you approach it. Because leadership development is a process, there are ups and downs and successes and mistakes. Navigating this rollercoaster with openness to learning is crucial. Particularly when you take on new experiences and operate on your edge, you won't get everything right the first time you attempt something. We think this is a good thing! In fact, most of our leadership learning and development has been through facing trials and tribulations. Approaching development with a positive attitude and asking "What can I learn from this situation and how can I grow?" is much more effective than having a negative or defeatist attitude.

Ten Concrete Ways to Develop EIL

Building on the focus of relationships, experiences, and attitudes discussed above, we have identified ten concrete ways you can develop your EIL—many of which you can implement in the short term (e.g., today, this week, or this month).

1. *Locate and meet with a mentor who exemplifies the facet or capacity.* Seek out a well-respected leader such as a professor or coach. The relationship does not have to be long-term—it may simply

consist of a couple of lunches or conversations in which you learn more about the individual's perspective on the topic and what that person did to master that facet or capacity.

2. *Read an article or book on the facet or capacity.* A book or article is a perfect way to learn more about the capacity you want to develop. Plenty of research has been conducted on each of the facets and capacities, and we have identified resources for you in the chapters of this *Student Workbook.* Although gaining knowledge is not enough to effectively engage in leadership, it is an integral part of the development process.

3. *Join a student organization or place yourself in situations that require you to practice the facet or capacity.* As we mention in our book *Emotionally Intelligent Leadership: A Guide for Students,* we feel that school provides a wonderful "practice field" for learning about leadership. Student organizations, on-campus jobs, residence halls, project teams, workplaces, and the larger campus community are all potential practice fields for those interested in developing their leadership and making a difference in the lives of others. Getting involved or taking on a formal or informal leadership role is a great way to get to learn, observe, plan, and exercise any of the EIL facets or capacities.

4. *Take part in formal learning opportunities, retreats, or courses that focus on the facet or capacity.* It is likely that you can find courses on campus touching on topics such as team development, small-group communication, organizational communication, diversity, counseling psychology, sociology, management, organizational change, and leadership. Further, many campuses and schools offer leadership development opportunities in co-curricular (e.g., out-of-the-classroom) settings through leadership workshop series, retreats, or other learning experiences. By learning about the facet or capacity

from a variety of perspectives, you are better prepared to put the theory into practice.

5. *Blog or journal about the process of developing the facet or capacity.* Writing and reflecting on your experience is an important part of the learning process. The key is to reflect on the facet or capacity you hope to develop. Think about it the next time you exercise. Talk about it with a friend as you walk to class. What systems can you put in place to help you remember that this capacity is your focus? It may be as simple as writing the facet or capacity on the top of your planner, or putting a note on your mirror or a note in your phone.

6. *Have coffee or otherwise connect with others working on the same facet or capacity and talk about your experiences.* As with the preceding suggestion, you may need to get creative. But there's no denying you will have a better chance of success in mastering a facet or capacity if you collaborate with others in the effort. We understand that there probably is not an "EIL group" on campus, but there are people with whom you could connect who are likely seeking to develop their leadership capacities.

7. *Write a vision statement or story about a future positive state as it relates to the facet or capacity.* Visualizing a future state can be a powerful tool; simply ask any high-performing artist or athlete. So what do you see? What will change as you master this facet or capacity? How will that benefit you? How will others perceive you and how will that help you when leading others? We like the way author and futurist Joel Barker (1991) puts it: "Vision without action is merely a dream. Action without vision just passes time. Vision with action changes the world."

8. *Participate in opportunities to teach others about the facet or capacity.* At first this may seem unrealistic, but when you think about it, you'll realize that opportunities to teach others are all around you. This may be a class presentation, group project, service-learning project, or a coaching or mentoring

opportunity. Talk with others about what you are learning and why it is important. As Confucius suggested, "What I hear I forget. What I see I remember. What I do I understand." Teaching is the highest form of learning.

9. *Complete an assessment or instrument that can help you learn more about yourself.* The career center, the student life office, the counseling center, and even the library may have resources and assessments to assist you in developing your self-awareness. Take some time to investigate what's available. Assessments like the *EILS: Inventory*, the DiSC, StrengthsFinder, Myers-Briggs Type Indicator (MBTI), or Strong Interest Inventory are good places to start.

10. *Find a job or internship that will require you to use (and practice) the facet or capacity.* What jobs or internships will challenge you to use and develop EIL on a consistent basis? For instance, serving as a coach, camp counselor, tutor, or mentor will force you to demonstrate your leadership and develop any number of facets and capacities on a consistent basis.

Since the first edition of the *Emotionally Intelligent Leadership for Students: Workbook*, we have heard from colleagues and students that the resource was a very useful tool for the application of the concepts of EIL to students' lives. We developed the *Student Workbook* with the goals of providing learning opportunities that allow students to delve further into EIL, reflect upon how the concepts relate to their experiences, think critically, and apply the concepts to activities, case studies, and their own lives. In this second edition of the *Workbook* we have these same goals in mind.

Simply put, we believe more than ever that EIL has the potential to make a difference in leadership development. For students and young adults, EIL provides a framework, a toolbox, and a guide for seeing in themselves their unique capacity to make a difference in the lives of others. The *Student Workbook* provides a range of activities that engage multiple learning styles to accomplish this purpose.

The *Student Workbook* is aligned with the *Emotionally Intelligent Leadership for Students: Facilitation and Activity Guide*, which is used by leadership educators in a variety of curricular and co-curricular settings. We recognize, though, that some students may seek to delve further into EIL on their own and without a formal leadership course or program. Thus, a majority of the activities here can be completed on their own. The experiences and outcomes of completing an activity may be different based on whether they are completed as part of a module from the *Facilitation and Activity Guide* or on their own, but we are confident that regardless of the context, they will be useful in helping students in their leadership learning and development. We have noted throughout the *Student Workbook* the specific activities that will not make sense as stand-alone experiences and those that must be tied to an activity from the *Facilitation and Activity Guide*. In addition to pairing with the *Facilitation and Activity Guide*, the *Student Workbook* is a great companion resource to the primary text, *Emotionally Intelligent Leadership: A Guide for Students* or in conjunction with the *Emotionally Intelligent Leadership for Students: Inventory*. These different resources are discussed in more detail following.

The *Student Workbook* is part of a series of companion resources that supports the primary text *Emotionally Intelligent Leadership: A Guide for Students*. We think of these resources as a suite of offerings that provide direct, hands-on learning experiences. The second edition suite consists of four separate but interrelated resources:

- *Emotionally Intelligent Leadership: A Guide for Students*—The primary text that introduces EIL and explores each facet and capacity

- *Emotionally Intelligent Leadership for Students: Inventory*—A self-assessment that illuminates how a person demonstrates EIL
- *Emotionally Intelligent Leadership for Students: Facilitation and Activity Guide*—A collection of learning activities to teach and facilitate the EIL facets and capacities
- *Emotionally Intelligent Leadership for Students: Student Workbook*—A collection of insights on the facets and capacities, self-guided activities, and additional resources that guide individual learning

We now offer brief descriptions of the resources.

Emotionally Intelligent Leadership: A Guide for Students

Emotionally Intelligent Leadership: A Guide for Students, Second Edition is a groundbreaking book that combines the concepts of emotional intelligence (EI) and leadership in one model: emotionally intelligent leadership. This important resource offers students a practical guide for developing their EIL capacities and emphasizes that leadership is a learnable skill that is based on developing healthy and effective relationships. Step by step, we outline the EIL model of three facets (consciousness of context, consciousness of self, and consciousness of others) and explore the nineteen capacities that define emotionally intelligent leadership.

The *Inventory*

One of the greatest challenges in student leadership development is translating theory into practice—how do the big ideas about leadership make sense to us as individuals so that we can behave differently? The starting point for changing behavior is changing thinking. Assessments serve many purposes, and one purpose we find incredibly compelling is that assessments give us a chance to see ourselves in a particular light. Looking intentionally at ourselves through the lens of EIL provides a unique opportunity to make meaningful connections between ideas and ourselves. The *Inventory* is a bridge—from theory to practice, from abstract ideas to concrete experiences, from thinking to action.

The Inventory, Second Edition provides an opportunity to explore experiences in leadership with a focus on identifying strengths and areas for improvement based on past behaviors. At the same time, the *Inventory* advances the learning from the present into the future with a focus on self-improvement and leadership development. Results include an enhanced understanding of EIL and its application, identification of perceived strengths and limitations, and developing an action plan for further development.

The *Facilitation and Activity Guide*

The *Facilitation and Activity Guide, Second Edition* is written for leadership educators and practitioners, campus-based professionals, faculty, and anyone interested in guiding students and young adults through hands-on learning opportunities that deepen their understanding of emotionally intelligent leadership. The *Facilitation and Activity Guide* is organized in a similar fashion to *Emotionally Intelligent Leadership: A Guide for Students*, with chapters dedicated to each of the three facets (consciousness of context, consciousness of self, consciousness of others) and to the nineteen capacities of EIL. Within each chapter are multiple modules that outline ways to explore, learn, and/or practice the particular facet or capacity of interest. Each module outlines everything a facilitator needs to know to prepare and facilitate the learning experience. The modules range in duration from 10 to 80 minutes. Within each module is an overview of the activities that will be facilitated with learning objectives, written directions, talking points, and discussion questions. When additional materials are needed, they are listed at the outset. When supplemental activity sheets are referenced, they are found in the *Student Workbook* so that the students may use this book as an additional resource during the course of the learning experience.

The *Student Workbook*

Recognizing the need for students to actively engage in their learning, the *Student Workbook, Second Edition* supports and complements the material covered in the *Facilitation and Activity Guide* and the *Inventory*. The *Student Workbook* is designed to be used in conjunction with the *Facilitation and Activity Guide*, as a follow-up to the *Inventory*, or as a companion resource for the book itself. Activities referenced in the *Facilitation and Activity Guide* are included in the *Student Workbook*. The *Student Workbook* presents the reader with interactive activities that stimulate additional integration of the material presented, as well as case studies, questions for further reflection, and additional resources for further learning. Each chapter of the *Student Workbook* follows the flow of the book and the *Facilitation and Activity Guide*.

In Closing

A Chinese proverb reads "Tell me and I forget. Show me and I remember. Involve me and I understand." In our experiences as educators and as leaders, we strongly believe that one can truly develop one's leadership ability only through hard work, deliberate practice, and finding ways to apply leadership concepts to one's life. In other words, you must involve yourself in leadership. This *Student Workbook* provides you with opportunities to do just that. We invite you to reflect, engage, and dig deep.

Dive In!

> How wonderful it is that nobody need wait a single moment before starting to improve the world.
>
> —*Anne Frank*

We absolutely agree with Anne Frank. We all have the capacity to improve the world, and our ability to do so depends in great part on our self-work. Every day we have a choice in how to direct our time and energy. We encourage you to identify ways to continually develop and grow. We have identified a number of strategies in this chapter, and your first step is to dive into this workbook and engage with the EIL model.

Reference

Barker, J. (1991). *The power of vision (VHS)*. United States: Starthrower Distribution.

Marcy Levy Shankman, PhD
Scott J. Allen, PhD
Paige Haber-Curran, PhD

ACKNOWLEDGMENTS

We are indebted to the team at Jossey-Bass: Erin Null, our wonderful editor, who is truly a partner in our work; Alison Knowles, associate editor; and Cathy Mallon, senior production editor. Together, they have worked collaboratively with us along each step of the way, pushing when we needed to be pushed and encouraging us to pause when we needed that important voice of reason. To Erin, especially, we appreciate your openness, interest in advancing the work, and stable hand that brings clarity and thoughtfulness to the work.

Finally, we are thankful that we have partners and families who are patient and always supportive—they keep us grounded and remind us of why we do the work that we do.

ABOUT THE AUTHORS

Marcy Levy Shankman, PhD, has been training and consulting in leadership development and organizational effectiveness since 1998. She is vice president for strategy and director of Leadership Cleveland at the Cleveland Leadership Center. In this role she works with leaders from a cross-section of Cleveland's community to advance their civic engagement and leadership development. Marcy is also principal of MLS Consulting LLC, which she founded in 2001. Marcy focuses on facilitating strategic planning and visioning initiatives, organizational change and development projects, as well as leadership training and board development.

Throughout her career, Marcy has spoken professionally and written in peer-reviewed journals and professional publications on leadership, emotional intelligence, and organizational effectiveness. Her focus is on helping students of all ages, from high school students to senior-level executives, to consider ways to enhance their leadership capacity.

Marcy teaches in the Non-Profit Administration Program as an instructor at John Carroll University. Marcy earned her PhD from Indiana University in higher education and student affairs, her master's in college student personnel from the University of Maryland, and her bachelor's from William and Mary in religion and anthropology. Marcy is an active volunteer and lives in Shaker Heights, Ohio, with her husband, Brett, and two children, Rebecca and Joshua.

Scott J. Allen, PhD, is an associate professor of management at John Carroll University. In 2008 and 2013, Scott was voted outstanding teacher in the Boler School of Business, and he enjoys working with students of all ages. Scott earned his PhD in leadership and change from Antioch University, his master's in human resource development from Xavier University, and undergraduate degree in family social science from the University of Minnesota. His research interests include leadership development and emotionally intelligent leadership.

His research has been published in several academic journals, including the *Journal of Leadership Education*, the *Journal of Leadership Studies*, *Advances in Developing Human Resources*, and *SAM Advanced Management Journal*. Scott is the coauthor of *The Little Book of Leadership Development* and *A Charge Nurse's Guide: Navigating the Path of Leadership*.

In addition to teaching and writing, Scott conducts workshops, leads retreats, and consults across industries. Scott is a member of the Academy of Management and the Association of Leadership Educators. He serves on the boards of the International Leadership Association, OBTS Teaching Society for Management Educators, and Beta Theta Pi Fraternity. He lives in Chagrin Falls, Ohio, with his wife, Jessica, and three children, Will, Kate, and Emily.

Paige Haber-Curran, PhD, is assistant professor for the Student Affairs in Higher Education master's program at Texas State University. In 2014 Paige was recognized with the Presidential Award for Excellence in Teaching at Texas State University. She also serves as the program coordinator for the program. Paige earned her PhD in leadership studies from the University of San Diego, her master's degree in college student personnel from the University of Maryland, and undergraduate degrees in business management and German studies from the University of Arizona.

Paige's research interests include college student leadership development, emotionally intelligent leadership, women and leadership, and gender in higher education. Her work has been published in several academic journals, including the *Journal of Leadership Education*, *NASPA Journal about Women in Higher Education*, and *Educational Action Research*. She also has published a number of practitioner-focused chapters in books including *The Handbook for Student Leadership Development*, *Emerging Issues and Practices in Peer Education*, and *Exploring Leadership Facilitation and Activity Guide*. Paige is co-editor of the forthcoming book *Advancing Women and Leadership Theory*. In 2013 she was selected as an Emerging Scholar for ACPA: College Student Educators International. Paige consults and speaks around the world on topics of leadership.

Paige is actively involved in ACPA: College Student Educators International and the International Leadership Association (ILA). She also serves as a Co-Lead Facilitator for the LeaderShape Institute. Paige lives in Austin, Texas, with her husband, Tom, and their Portuguese Water Dogs, Ike and Murphy.

To contact the authors:

Marcy Levy Shankman: shankman@mlsconsulting.net
Scott J. Allen: sallen@jcu.edu
Paige Haber-Curran: paige.haber@gmail.com

emotionally intelligent leadership

for Students

Chapter 1   Introduction to Emotionally Intelligent Leadership

Activities

1.1 EIL Snapshot

Emotionally Intelligent Leadership Defined

Emotionally intelligent leadership (EIL) promotes an intentional focus on three facets: consciousness of self, consciousness of others, and consciousness of context. Across the three EIL facets are nineteen capacities that equip individuals with the knowledge, skills, perspectives, and attitudes to achieve desired leadership outcomes.

Emotionally Intelligent Leadership

Emotionally intelligent leadership is integrative in nature (Boyer, 1990). In other words, we have combined what we believe is the best thinking on emotional intelligence and leadership into one model. For a more academic and theoretical introduction to the model, see Allen, Shankman, and Miguel (2012). In the development of EIL we have drawn upon three sources: our own experiences, the experiences of students with whom we have worked, and the literature and scholarship on emotional intelligence and leadership.

In the midst of all this, however, we emphasize the great value your own experiences and perspectives hold. You need to determine your own styles and approaches to leadership. We note throughout the book that intentionality around your own development is central to enhancing EIL. In other words, just as with any other skill or ability, you have to *want* to develop it. Effective leadership takes commitment and awareness. Effective leadership requires changing behavior. Effective leadership takes deliberate practice.

EIL synthesizes two major bodies of research and theory: emotional intelligence and leadership. In 1990, Peter Salovey and John Mayer published a paper in which they coined the term *emotional intelligence* (EI) and defined it as "the ability to monitor one's own and others' feelings and emotions to use the information to guide one's thinking and actions" (p. 189). In 1995, Daniel Goleman (2000) made EI popular in his book *Emotional Intelligence* and described it as the ability "to recognize and regulate emotions in ourselves and others" (p. 2). We believe EI is at the core of effective leadership.

As such, emotionally intelligent leadership (EIL) promotes an intentional focus on three facets: consciousness of self, consciousness of others, and consciousness of context. Across the three EIL facets are nineteen capacities that equip individuals with the knowledge, skills, perspectives, and attitudes to achieve desired leadership outcomes.

The Three Facets of Emotionally Intelligent Leadership

Central to our definition of EIL are the three facets: consciousness of self, consciousness of others, and consciousness of context. Embedded in our assumptions about leadership is our belief that leadership is not solely about the leader—leadership is a reciprocal relationship with others that aims to effect positive change. Equally important, but often not recognized clearly, is that the context in which the work is being done is fundamental to success or failure. Following is how we define each of the three facets.

1. *Consciousness of Self:* Demonstrating emotionally intelligent leadership involves awareness of your abilities, emotions, and perceptions. Consciousness of self is about prioritizing the inner work of reflection and introspection, and appreciating that self-awareness is a continual and ongoing process.

2. *Consciousness of Others:* Demonstrating emotionally intelligent leadership involves awareness of the abilities, emotions, and perceptions of others. Consciousness of others is about intentionally working with and influencing individuals and groups to bring about positive change.

3. *Consciousness of Context:* Demonstrating emotionally intelligent leadership involves awareness of the setting and situation. Consciousness of context is about paying attention to how environmental factors and internal group dynamics affect the process of leadership.

When discussing the three facets, we use the metaphor of *signal strength* (see Figure 1.1). In the context of cellular communication and Wi-Fi networking, signal strength is something many of us are attuned to each day—after all, the strength of our signal determines our ability to connect and communicate with others to accomplish our desired tasks and goals.

Here's how the metaphor works: imagine yourself as the dot. Each bar that radiates out from you represents the three facets (self, others, context—in that order). With one bar (consciousness of self), you will have a certain level of success. Add one more bar, your signal strength increases because you are in tune with yourself and others (consciousness of others). Signal strength cannot be

Figure 1.1   Signal Strength

maximized, however, until all three bars are working at full capacity. Adding the third bar means you are also conscious of the larger context. When you are conscious of self, others, and context, we call this working at full strength.

Now, just like the Wi-Fi network signal strength changes, so does our capacity to demonstrate EIL. Each of us moves in and out of "hot spots." In some cases we may be left with low to no signal because we are not paying attention to ourselves, others, or the context. This would result in limiting our ability to connect. In other words, any time we find ourselves in a new context, if we're not paying attention, we may find ourselves without the knowledge, skills, and abilities to succeed. The opposite is also true—when we are fully aware, maximizing our capacities, then all three bars are "lit up" and we are at full strength.

As you think about leadership, and EIL in particular, remember this simple image and metaphor. Are you working at full signal strength, or are you focused only on self? Leadership is best demonstrated when working at full signal. Your ability to monitor all three facets intentionally will help you to lead effectively. Anyone committed to leadership must be aware of himself or herself; the needs, interests, and abilities of others involved; and factors from the larger environment and the group that come into play.

The Nineteen Capacities of EIL

Now that we have you thinking about the three facets of EIL, you may be wondering what those facets look like in action. EIL consists of nineteen capacities that are inherent in the three facets. The *American Heritage Dictionary* defines *capacity* as "ability to perform or produce; capability." We chose this word because we believe everyone has the capacity to engage in leadership. We believe that each of the EIL capacities is learnable and teachable. Refer to the appendix for complete definitions of the nineteen capacities of EIL.

 Consciousness of Self

Emotional self-perception: Identifying emotions and their influence on behavior
Emotional self-control: Consciously moderating emotions
Authenticity: Being transparent and trustworthy
Healthy self-esteem: Having a balanced sense of self
Flexibility: Being open and adaptive to change
Optimism: Having a positive outlook
Initiative: Taking action
Achievement: Striving for excellence

 Consciousness of Others

Displaying empathy: Being emotionally in tune with others
Inspiring others: Energizing individuals and groups
Coaching others: Enhancing the skills and abilities of others
Capitalizing on difference: Benefiting from multiple perspectives
Developing relationships: Building a network of trusting relationships
Building teams: Working with others to accomplish a shared purpose
Demonstrating citizenship: Fulfilling responsibilities to the group
Managing conflict: Identifying and resolving conflict
Facilitating change: Working toward new directions

Consciousness of Context

Analyzing the group: Interpreting group dynamics
Assessing the environment: Interpreting external forces and trends

When we think of effective leadership, we envision a healthy and appropriate balance of these capacities. As we have discussed, there is no fixed formula for which capacities you must demonstrate and when; that would minimize the complexities and realities of leadership. We also know that nineteen capacities can feel overwhelming. We are not claiming that you have to be excellent in all nineteen capacities; rather, we all have the nineteen capacities at our disposal to use and develop. Consider the metaphor of an orchestra. The nineteen capacities are the different instruments in the orchestra—some may come into play in some situations more than others (e.g., louder or for longer sets), but for a full concert, it is likely each instrument needs to be present at some level. So, while in a certain situation, we may only need to intentionally use a core set of seven EIL capacities, we have nineteen to choose from.

As stated previously, effective leadership is about having an appropriate balance among the capacities. It is not effective or advisable to demonstrate any one of these capacities to excess. Any strength taken to an extreme can become a limitation. At the same time, underusing any capacity can also have negative repercussions. For instance, with too much emphasis on *building teams*, a group can become bogged down, even paralyzed, thus keeping the team from progressing and moving forward. At the other extreme, if *building teams* is ignored, people can feel alienated. This often results in one person from the group doing all the work.

The bottom line is to make sure that the balance is dynamic—it is continually shifting based on the context. In other words, the appropriate demonstration or use of a capacity in one situation may be inadequate in another situation, based on the individual, the group, and the context. That's one of the reasons why EIL is composed of both the facets (paying attention to what is happening) and the capacities (doing what is needed).

References

Allen, S. J., Shankman, M. L., & Miguel, R. (2012). Emotionally intelligent leadership: An integrative, process-oriented theory of student leadership. *Journal of Leadership Education, 11*(1), 177–203.

Boyer, E. (1990). *Scholarship reconsidered: Priorities of the professoriate.* (Eric Document Reproduction Service No. ED326149).

Goleman, D. (1995). *Emotional intelligence.* New York, NY: Bantam Books.

Goleman, D. (2000). Leadership that gets results. *Harvard Business Review*, March–April, 78–90.

Salovey, P., & Mayer, J. D. (1990). Emotional intelligence. *Imagination, Cognition, and Personality, 9*(3), 185–211.

Activity 1.1: EIL Snapshot

Think about a formal or informal leadership role you have played and keep this in mind as you assess yourself on the following items. A formal leadership role may be a position you held in an organization or on a team (president or co-captain) or an informal role is one you played in a group (e.g., helped with some aspect of a project, led a team for a class project). With this context and role in mind, assess *yourself* on the EIL facets and capacities below.

Consciousness of Self

Being aware of yourself in terms of your abilities, emotions, and perceptions

| 1 | 2 | 3 | 4 | 5 |
| Low Capacity | | | | High Capacity |

Emotional Self-Perception

Identifying emotions and their influence on behavior

| 1 | 2 | 3 | 4 | 5 |
| Low Capacity | | | | High Capacity |

Emotional Self-Control

Consciously moderating emotions

| 1 | 2 | 3 | 4 | 5 |
| Low Capacity | | | | High Capacity |

Authenticity

Being transparent and trustworthy

| 1 | 2 | 3 | 4 | 5 |
| Low Capacity | | | | High Capacity |

Copyright © 2015 John Wiley and Sons, Inc. For use in Workbook only. Not to be reproduced without permission.

Healthy Self-Esteem

Having a balanced sense of self

	1	2	3	4	5
	Low Capacity				High Capacity

Flexibility

Being open and adaptive to change

	1	2	3	4	5
	Low Capacity				High Capacity

Optimism

Having a positive outlook

	1	2	3	4	5
	Low Capacity				High Capacity

Initiative

Taking action

	1	2	3	4	5
	Low Capacity				High Capacity

Achievement

Striving for excellence

	1	2	3	4	5
	Low Capacity				High Capacity

Copyright © 2015 John Wiley and Sons, Inc. For use in Workbook only. Not to be reproduced without permission.

Consciousness of Others

Being aware of the abilities, emotions, and perceptions of others

1	2	3	4	5
Low Capacity				High Capacity

Displaying Empathy

Being emotionally in tune with others

1	2	3	4	5
Low Capacity				High Capacity

Inspiring Others

Energizing individuals and groups

1	2	3	4	5
Low Capacity				High Capacity

Coaching Others

Enhancing the skills and abilities of others

1	2	3	4	5
Low Capacity				High Capacity

Capitalizing on Difference

Benefiting from multiple perspectives

1	2	3	4	5
Low Capacity				High Capacity

Copyright © 2015 John Wiley and Sons, Inc. For use in Workbook only. Not to be reproduced without permission.

Developing Relationships

Building a network of trusting relationships

1	2	3	4	5
Low Capacity				High Capacity

Building Teams

Working with others to accomplish a shared purpose

1	2	3	4	5
Low Capacity				High Capacity

Demonstrating Citizenship

Fulfilling responsibilities to the group

1	2	3	4	5
Low Capacity				High Capacity

Managing Conflict

Identifying and resolving conflict

1	2	3	4	5
Low Capacity				High Capacity

Facilitating Change

Working toward new directions

1	2	3	4	5
Low Capacity				High Capacity

Copyright © 2015 John Wiley and Sons, Inc. For use in Workbook only. Not to be reproduced without permission.

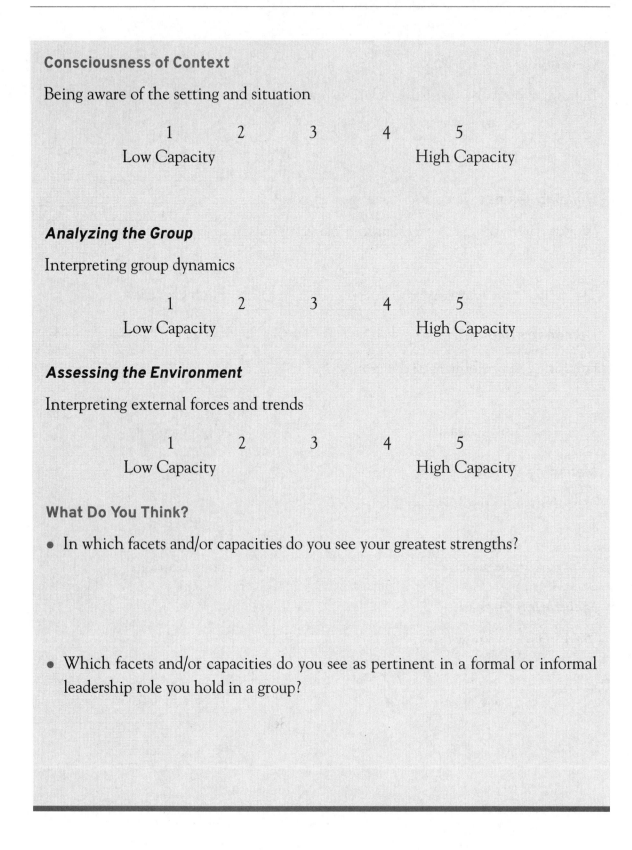

Consciousness of Context

Being aware of the setting and situation

1	2	3	4	5
Low Capacity				High Capacity

Analyzing the Group

Interpreting group dynamics

1	2	3	4	5
Low Capacity				High Capacity

Assessing the Environment

Interpreting external forces and trends

1	2	3	4	5
Low Capacity				High Capacity

What Do You Think?

- In which facets and/or capacities do you see your greatest strengths?

- Which facets and/or capacities do you see as pertinent in a formal or informal leadership role you hold in a group?

Copyright © 2015 John Wiley and Sons, Inc. For use in Workbook only. Not to be reproduced without permission.

Chapter 2   Consciousness of Self

Activities

Consciousness of Self Defined

Demonstrating emotionally intelligent leadership involves awareness of your abilities, emotions, and perceptions. Consciousness of self is about prioritizing the inner work of reflection and introspection and appreciating that self-awareness is a continual and ongoing process.

Online Articles and Resources

- Consortium for Research on Emotional Intelligence in Organizations: www.eiconsortium.org
- Emotional Intelligence: Self-Awareness: www.leadershipnow.com
- Emotional intelligence information: www.unh.edu/emotional_intelligence
- Internet directory on emotional intelligence: www.eq.org

- Self-Awareness and the Effective Leader: www.inc.com
- Personal website of scholar Reuven Bar-On: www.reuvenbaron.org
- Six Seconds: www.6seconds.org

Suggested Books

- *The Artist's Way Workbook* by Julia Cameron
- *Beyond Effective: Practices in Self-Aware Leadership* by David Peck
- *The Enneagram Made Easy: Discover the Nine Types of People* by Renee Baron and Elizabeth Wagele
- *An Essay Concerning Human Understanding* by John Locke (accessible through Google Books)
- *Journal to the Self: Twenty-Two Paths to Personal Growth—Open the Door to Self-Understanding by Writing, Reading, and Creating a Journal of Your Life* by Kathleen Adams
- *The Leadership Challenge Workbook* by James M. Kouzes and Barry Z. Posner
- *Learning to Lead: A Workbook on Becoming a Leader* by Warren Bennis
- *Let Your Life Speak* by Parker Palmer
- *Personality Plus: How to Understand Others by Understanding Yourself* by Florence Littauer
- *Principle-Centered Leadership* by Stephen R. Covey
- *Waking Up to Resonance and Renewal: Charting a Path to Self-Awareness and Great Leadership* by Richard E. Boyatzis and Annie McKee
- *What Type Am I? The Myers-Briggs Type Indicator Made Easy* by Renee Baron

Suggested Television Series

The following television shows highlight the facet of consciousness of self. Some characters may overuse this facet; others may lack the ability to use it successfully.

- *The Fashion Show/Project Runway*
- *Lost*
- *Modern Family*
- *The Office*
- *The Oprah Winfrey Show*
- *The Real World*
- *Seinfeld*
- *30 Rock*
- *Top Chef*

Notable Quotes

O, happy the soul that saw its own faults.
—*Rumi, poet and philosopher*

The authentic self is the soul made visible.
—*Sarah Ban Breathnach*

Everything that irritates us about others can lead us to an understanding of ourselves.
—*Carl Jung, psychologist*

Everyone thinks of changing the world, but no one thinks of changing himself.
—*Leo Tolstoy, author*

I think self-awareness is probably the most important thing towards being a champion.

    —*Billie Jean King, tennis player*

To have greater self-awareness or understanding means to have a better grasp of reality.

    —*The Dalai Lama, spiritual leader*

Being cool is being your own self, not doing something that someone else is telling you to do.

    —*Vanessa Hudgens, actress*

Activity 2.1: Consciousness of Self #1

Directions: Read the definition of consciousness of self and the eight capacities that bring this facet to life. As you read the definitions of the eight capacities, circle key words and phrases that stand out to you.

Consciousness of Self

Demonstrating emotionally intelligent leadership involves awareness of your abilities, emotions, and perceptions. Consciousness of self is about prioritizing the inner work of reflection and introspection, and appreciating that self-awareness is a continual and ongoing process.

1. *Emotional self-perception:* <u>Identifying emotions and their influence on behavior</u>. Emotional self-perception is about describing, naming, and understanding your emotions. Emotionally intelligent leaders are aware of how situations influence emotions and how emotions affect interactions with others.

2. *Emotional self-control:* <u>Consciously moderating emotions</u>. Emotional self-control means intentionally managing your emotions and understanding how and when to demonstrate them appropriately. Emotionally intelligent leaders take responsibility for regulating their emotions and are not victims of them.

3. *Authenticity:* <u>Being transparent and trustworthy</u>. Authenticity is about developing credibility, being transparent, and aligning words with actions. Emotionally intelligent leaders live their values and present themselves and their motives in an open and honest manner.

Copyright © 2015 John Wiley and Sons, Inc. For use in Workbook only. Not to be reproduced without permission.

4. *Healthy self-esteem:* <u>Having a balanced sense of self</u>. Healthy self-esteem is about balancing confidence in your abilities with humility. Emotionally intelligent leaders are resilient and remain confident when faced with setbacks and challenges.

5. *Flexibility:* <u>Being open and adaptive to change</u>. Flexibility is about adapting your approach and style based on changing circumstances. Emotionally intelligent leaders seek input and feedback from others and adjust accordingly.

6. *Optimism:* <u>Having a positive outlook</u>. Optimism is about setting a positive tone for the future. Emotionally intelligent leaders use optimism to foster hope and generate energy.

7. *Initiative:* <u>Taking action</u>. Initiative means being a self-starter and being motivated to take the first step. Emotionally intelligent leaders are ready to take action, demonstrate interest, and capitalize on opportunities.

8. *Achievement:* <u>Striving for excellence</u>. Achievement is about setting high personal standards and getting results. Emotionally intelligent leaders strive to improve and are motivated by an internal drive to succeed.

Copyright © 2015 John Wiley and Sons, Inc. For use in Workbook only. Not to be reproduced without permission.

Activity 2.2: Personal SWOT

Directions: SWOT stands for *strengths*, *weaknesses*, *opportunities*, and *threats*. For each of the capacities of consciousness of self, consider your strengths, weaknesses, opportunities, and threats by answering the prompts provided.

Emotional Self-Perception: <u>Identifying emotions and their influence on behavior.</u> Emotional self-perception is about describing, naming, and understanding your emotions. Emotionally intelligent leaders are aware of how situations influence emotions and how emotions affect interactions with others.

- *Strengths:* In what ways do you excel in this capacity?

- *Weaknesses:* In what ways do you need to develop and grow?

- *Opportunities:* What opportunities exist that you can take advantage of?

- *Threats:* What can get in the way of you excelling or further developing in this capacity?

Copyright © 2015 John Wiley and Sons, Inc. For use in Workbook only. Not to be reproduced without permission.

Emotional Self-Control: <u>Consciously moderating emotions</u>. Emotional self-control means intentionally managing your emotions and understanding how and when to demonstrate them appropriately. Emotionally intelligent leaders take responsibility for regulating their emotions and are not victims of them.

- *Strengths:* In what ways do you excel in this capacity?

- *Weaknesses:* In what ways do you need to develop and grow?

- *Opportunities:* What opportunities exist that you can take advantage of?

- *Threats:* What can get in the way of you excelling or further developing in this capacity?

Copyright © 2015 John Wiley and Sons, Inc. For use in Workbook only. Not to be reproduced without permission.

Authenticity: <u>Being transparent and trustworthy.</u> Authenticity is about developing credibility, being transparent, and aligning words with actions. Emotionally intelligent leaders live their values and present themselves and their motives in an open and honest manner.

- *Strengths:* In what ways do you excel in this capacity?

- *Weaknesses:* In what ways do you need to develop and grow?

- *Opportunities:* What opportunities exist that you can take advantage of?

- *Threats:* What can get in the way of you excelling or further developing in this capacity?

Copyright © 2015 John Wiley and Sons, Inc. For use in Workbook only. Not to be reproduced without permission.

Healthy Self-Esteem: <u>Having a balanced sense of self</u>. Healthy self-esteem is about balancing confidence in your abilities with humility. Emotionally intelligent leaders are resilient and remain confident when faced with setbacks and challenges.

- *Strengths:* In what ways do you excel in this capacity?

- *Weaknesses:* In what ways do you need to develop and grow?

- *Opportunities:* What opportunities exist that you can take advantage of?

- *Threats:* What can get in the way of you excelling or further developing in this capacity?

Copyright © 2015 John Wiley and Sons, Inc. For use in Workbook only. Not to be reproduced without permission.

Flexibility: <u>Being open and adaptive to change</u>. Flexibility is about adapting your approach and style based on changing circumstances. Emotionally intelligent leaders seek input and feedback from others and adjust accordingly.

- *Strengths:* In what ways do you excel in this capacity?

- *Weaknesses:* In what ways do you need to develop and grow?

- *Opportunities:* What opportunities exist that you can take advantage of?

- *Threats:* What can get in the way of you excelling or further developing in this capacity?

Copyright © 2015 John Wiley and Sons, Inc. For use in Workbook only. Not to be reproduced without permission.

Optimism: <u>Having a positive outlook</u>. Optimism is about setting a positive tone for the future. Emotionally intelligent leaders use optimism to foster hope and generate energy.

- *Strengths:* In what ways do you excel in this capacity?

- *Weaknesses:* In what ways do you need to develop and grow?

- *Opportunities:* What opportunities exist that you can take advantage of?

- *Threats:* What can get in the way of you excelling or further developing in this capacity?

Copyright © 2015 John Wiley and Sons, Inc. For use in Workbook only. Not to be reproduced without permission.

Initiative: <u>Taking action</u>. Initiative means being a self-starter and being motivated to take the first step. Emotionally intelligent leaders are ready to take action, demonstrate interest, and capitalize on opportunities.

- *Strengths:* In what ways do you excel in this capacity?

- *Weaknesses:* In what ways do you need to develop and grow?

- *Opportunities:* What opportunities exist that you can take advantage of?

- *Threats:* What can get in the way of you excelling or further developing in this capacity?

Copyright © 2015 John Wiley and Sons, Inc. For use in Workbook only. Not to be reproduced without permission.

Achievement: <u>Striving for excellence</u>. Achievement is about setting high personal standards and getting results. Emotionally intelligent leaders strive to improve and are motivated by an internal drive to succeed.

- *Strengths:* In what ways do you excel in this capacity?

- *Weaknesses:* In what ways do you need to develop and grow?

- *Opportunities:* What opportunities exist that you can take advantage of?

- *Threats:* What can get in the way of you excelling or further developing in this capacity?

Copyright © 2015 John Wiley and Sons, Inc. For use in Workbook only. Not to be reproduced without permission.

Activity 2.3: Consciousness of Self #2

Note: This activity accompanies the *Famous Faces* module in the *Emotionally Intelligent Leadership for Students: Facilitation and Activity Guide*. See your facilitator for additional instructions.

Directions: Read the definition of consciousness of self and the eight capacities that bring this facet to life. As you read the definitions of the eight capacities, circle key words and phrases that stand out to you.

Consciousness of Self

Demonstrating emotionally intelligent leadership involves awareness of your abilities, emotions, and perceptions. Consciousness of self is about prioritizing the inner work of reflection and introspection, and appreciating that self-awareness is a continual and ongoing process.

1. *Emotional self-perception:* <u>Identifying emotions and their influence on behavior.</u> Emotional self-perception is about describing, naming, and understanding your emotions. Emotionally intelligent leaders are aware of how situations influence emotions and how emotions affect interactions with others.

2. *Emotional self-control:* <u>Consciously moderating emotions.</u> Emotional self-control means intentionally managing your emotions and understanding how and when to demonstrate them appropriately. Emotionally intelligent leaders take responsibility for regulating their emotions and are not victims of them.

3. *Authenticity:* <u>Being transparent and trustworthy.</u> Authenticity is about developing credibility, being transparent, and aligning words with actions. Emotionally intelligent leaders live their values and present themselves and their motives in an open and honest manner.

Copyright © 2015 John Wiley and Sons, Inc. For use in Workbook only. Not to be reproduced without permission.

4. *Healthy self-esteem:* <u>Having a balanced sense of self</u>. Healthy self-esteem is about balancing confidence in your abilities with humility. Emotionally intelligent leaders are resilient and remain confident when faced with setbacks and challenges.

5. *Flexibility:* <u>Being open and adaptive to change</u>. Flexibility is about adapting your approach and style based on changing circumstances. Emotionally intelligent leaders seek input and feedback from others and adjust accordingly.

6. *Optimism:* <u>Having a positive outlook</u>. Optimism is about setting a positive tone for the future. Emotionally intelligent leaders use optimism to foster hope and generate energy.

7. *Initiative:* <u>Taking action</u>. Initiative means being a self-starter and being motivated to take the first step. Emotionally intelligent leaders are ready to take action, demonstrate interest, and capitalize on opportunities.

8. *Achievement:* <u>Striving for excellence</u>. Achievement is about setting high personal standards and getting results. Emotionally intelligent leaders strive to improve and are motivated by an internal drive to succeed.

Copyright © 2015 John Wiley and Sons, Inc. For use in Workbook only. Not to be reproduced without permission.

Activity 2.4: Famous Faces Scale

Note: This activity accompanies the *Famous Faces* module in the *Emotionally Intelligent Leadership for Students: Facilitation and Activity Guide*. See your facilitator for additional instructions.

Directions: Rate each individual on his or her use of each of the eight capacities as you see each image. Rank each individual "underuse," "appropriate use," and "overuse" for each of the eight capacities listed in the table. If you do not know the leader displayed, indicate this with "N/A" or ask your facilitator.

Individual/Capacity	Underuse	Appropriate Use	Overuse
Person 1:			
1. Emotional Self-Perception			
2. Emotional Self-Control			
3. Healthy Self-Esteem			
4. Authenticity			
5. Flexibility			
6. Achievement			
7. Initiative			
8. Optimism			
Person 2:			
1. Emotional Self-Perception			
2. Emotional Self-Control			
3. Healthy Self-Esteem			
4. Authenticity			
5. Flexibility			
6. Achievement			
7. Initiative			
8. Optimism			

Copyright © 2015 John Wiley and Sons, Inc. For use in Workbook only. Not to be reproduced without permission.

Individual/Capacity	Underuse	Appropriate Use	Overuse
Person 3:			
1. Emotional Self-Perception			
2. Emotional Self-Control			
3. Healthy Self-Esteem			
4. Authenticity			
5. Flexibility			
6. Achievement			
7. Initiative			
8. Optimism			
Person 4:			
1. Emotional Self-Perception			
2. Emotional Self-Control			
3. Healthy Self-Esteem			
4. Authenticity			
5. Flexibility			
6. Achievement			
7. Initiative			
8. Optimism			

Copyright © 2015 John Wiley and Sons, Inc. For use in Workbook only. Not to be reproduced without permission.

Activity 2.5: Consciousness of Self #3

Note: This activity accompanies the *A Ranking Debate* module in the *Emotionally Intelligent Leadership for Students: Facilitation and Activity Guide*. See your facilitator for additional instructions.

Directions: Read the definition of consciousness of self and the eight capacities that bring this facet to life. As you read the definitions of the eight capacities, circle key words and phrases that stand out to you.

Consciousness of Self

Demonstrating emotionally intelligent leadership involves awareness of your abilities, emotions, and perceptions. Consciousness of self is about prioritizing the inner work of reflection and introspection, and appreciating that self-awareness is a continual and ongoing process.

1. *Emotional self-perception:* <u>Identifying emotions and their influence on behavior.</u> Emotional self-perception is about describing, naming, and understanding your emotions. Emotionally intelligent leaders are aware of how situations influence emotions and how emotions affect interactions with others.

2. *Emotional self-control:* <u>Consciously moderating emotions.</u> Emotional self-control means intentionally managing your emotions and understanding how and when to demonstrate them appropriately. Emotionally intelligent leaders take responsibility for regulating their emotions and are not victims of them.

3. *Authenticity:* <u>Being transparent and trustworthy.</u> Authenticity is about developing credibility, being transparent, and aligning words with actions. Emotionally intelligent leaders live their values and present themselves and their motives in an open and honest manner.

Copyright © 2015 John Wiley and Sons, Inc. For use in Workbook only. Not to be reproduced without permission.

4. *Healthy self-esteem:* <u>Having a balanced sense of self</u>. Healthy self-esteem is about balancing confidence in your abilities with humility. Emotionally intelligent leaders are resilient and remain confident when faced with setbacks and challenges.

5. *Flexibility:* <u>Being open and adaptive to change</u>. Flexibility is about adapting your approach and style based on changing circumstances. Emotionally intelligent leaders seek input and feedback from others and adjust accordingly.

6. *Optimism:* <u>Having a positive outlook</u>. Optimism is about setting a positive tone for the future. Emotionally intelligent leaders use optimism to foster hope and generate energy.

7. *Initiative:* <u>Taking action</u>. Initiative means being a self-starter and being motivated to take the first step. Emotionally intelligent leaders are ready to take action, demonstrate interest, and capitalize on opportunities.

8. *Achievement:* <u>Striving for excellence</u>. Achievement is about setting high personal standards and getting results. Emotionally intelligent leaders strive to improve and are motivated by an internal drive to succeed.

Copyright © 2015 John Wiley and Sons, Inc. For use in Workbook only. Not to be reproduced without permission.

Activity 2.6: Consciousness of Self Capacities Scale

!

Note: This activity accompanies the *A Ranking Debate* module in the *Emotionally Intelligent Leadership for Students: Facilitation and Activity Guide*. See your facilitator for additional instructions.

Directions: Based on the ranking activity just concluded, how would you rank your use of the eight consciousness of self capacities?

First, list the capacity rankings based on the group activity and then place an X in the box that best describes your behavior of each capacity.

Capacity Rank	Underuse	Appropriate Use	Overuse
1.			
2.			
3.			
4.			
5.			
6.			
7.			
8.			

Copyright © 2015 John Wiley and Sons, Inc. For use in Workbook only. Not to be reproduced without permission.

Chapter 3 Emotional Self-Perception

Emotional Self-Perception Defined

Identifying emotions and their influence on behavior.   Emotional self-perception is about describing, naming, and understanding your emotions. Emotionally intelligent leaders are aware of how situations influence emotions and how emotions affect interactions with others.

Using This Capacity

Appropriate use of this capacity changes depending on the setting and situation. However, we developed the following statements to provide a snapshot of what it *may* look like if someone is overusing or underusing this capacity. We then conducted focus groups with student leaders, and they vetted and added to the statements. A number of these statements are presented here.

Individuals who overuse this capacity may be perceived by others as:

- lost in their own self-analysis;
- spending a lot of energy on behaving in ways they think others want them to;
- having difficulty letting others in;

- people who are difficult to know;
- too focused on themselves and how they are feeling to recognize others;
- too calculated with how they handle emotions.

Individuals who underuse this capacity may be perceived by others as:

- demonstrating inappropriate, unproductive, or simply unhelpful behaviors;
- unaware of how their emotions impact others;
- not trustworthy or transparent;
- unemotional or extremely guarded;
- subject to mood swings or irrational behaviors or emotions.

Online Articles and Resources

- Consortium for Research on Emotional Intelligence in Organizations: www.eiconsortium.org
- Emotional intelligence information: www.unh.edu/emotional _intelligence
- Internet directory on emotional intelligence: www.eq.org
- Negative Emotions in Response to Daily Stress Take a Toll on Long-Term Mental Health: www.sciencedaily.com
- Personal website of scholar Reuven Bar-On: www.reuvenbaron .org
- Six Seconds: www.6seconds.org

Suggested Books

- *Becoming a Resonant Leader: Develop Your Emotional Intelligence, Renew Your Relationships, Sustain Your Effectiveness* by Richard E. Boyatzis, Fran Johnston, and Annie McKee
- *Don't Let Your Emotions Run Your Life: How Dialectical Behavior Therapy Can Put You in Control* by Scott Spradlin

- *The Practicing Mind: Bringing Discipline and Focus into Your Life* by Thomas Sterner
- *Primal Leadership: Learning to Lead with Emotional Intelligence* by Daniel Goleman, Richard E. Boyatzis, and Annie McKee
- *Raising Your Emotional Intelligence: A Practical Guide* by Jeanne S. Segal
- *Thoughts and Feelings: Taking Control of Your Moods and Your Life* by Matthew McKay, Martha David, and Patrick Fanning

Suggested Films

The following films highlight the capacity of emotional self-perception. Some characters may overuse this capacity; others may lack the ability to use it successfully. As you watch any of the following, try and diagnose which characters are overusing or underusing this capacity, and who may be displaying an appropriate balance.

- *Bridget Jones*
- *The Dark Knight*
- *Falling Down*
- *Finding Nemo*
- *Gandhi*
- *The Hurt Locker*
- *A League of Their Own*
- *Lord of the Rings* trilogy
- *Milk*
- *On Golden Pond*
- *Ordinary People*
- *Primary Colors*
- *Remember the Titans*
- *Sid and Nancy*
- *Spider-Man*
- *Wall Street*
- *The Wizard of Oz*

Notable Quotes

Doo-wop is special music to me because it's so straightforward and melody-driven and captures emotions.
—*Bruno Mars, entertainer*

Analysis gave me great freedom of emotions and fantastic confidence. I felt I had served my time as a puppet.
—*Hedy Lamarr, actress*

I want my boys to have an understanding of people's emotions, their insecurities, people's distress, and their hopes and dreams.
—*Diana, Princess of Wales*

Even before Watergate and his resignation, Nixon had inspired conflicting and passionate emotions.
—*Stephen Ambrose, historian and author*

Feelings or emotions are the universal language and are to be honored. They are the authentic expression of who you are at your deepest place.
—*Judith Wright, poet*

I could work out a lot of my emotions by going to class and dancing.
—*Suzanne Farrell, ballerina*

Activity 3.1: **Twenty Emotions**

Directions: Find a partner and go "into the field" to practice observing the emotions of others. With the list of emotions as a reference, the objective is to gather as many emotional sightings as possible (e.g., two women laughing). Identify at least fifteen demonstrations of various emotions listed in the table below.

Emotions Generally Viewed as Negative	Emotions Generally Viewed as Positive
1. Bored	1. Happy
2. Frustrated	2. Secure
3. Anxious	3. Relaxed
4. Scared	4. Pleased
5. Angry	5. Surprised
6. Helpless	6. Intrigued
7. Guilty	7. Cheerful
8. Stressed	8. Prideful
9. Sad	9. Loving
10. Disgusted	10. Joy

Copyright © 2015 John Wiley and Sons, Inc. For use in Workbook only. Not to be reproduced without permission.

Activity 3.2: Emotional Self-Perception Case Study

Directions: The purpose of this activity is for you to write a personal case study. Please change names, places, events, and other identifying information. This is an opportunity to write a realistic, one- to two-page case study on the capacity of emotional self-perception. The case should highlight a time when your lack of emotional self-perception negatively affected you and/or others. Feel free to use the list of emotions provided in the *Twenty Emotions* activity (*Student Workbook*, 3.1) to identify emotions that may spark ideas.

You will need to describe the situation and setting for your example. This may mean a short description of the organization (student organization, athletic team, workplace, etc.), living space (apartment, house, camp, etc.), or group (friends, family, neighbors, etc.). Remember to avoid identifying information. Highlight the important individuals (remember to use false names), explain the situation or dilemma, and conclude with questions for the reader to address. You may be sharing your case studies with others, so include only what you will feel comfortable sharing.

Copyright © 2015 John Wiley and Sons, Inc. For use in Workbook only. Not to be reproduced without permission.

Activity 3.3: Twenty Emotions: Environment

Directions: This activity challenges you to think about emotions in your environment through a scavenger hunt activity. Use the checklist below to identify the various emotions displayed in the physical climate of an organization or a location with great meaning to you (e.g., the institution, an organization, an office space, a classroom). You need to identify *objects* in the environment that correspond with the emotions provided below. Then, to conclude you will examine the various objects you identified and assign an overall positivity score for the environment you have chosen (between 1 and 10, with 10 being a positive or uplifting environment).

Name of Organization _____

Negative Emotions	Object	Positive Emotions	Object
1. Bored		1. Happy	
2. Frustrated		2. Secure	
3. Anxious		3. Relaxed	
4. Scared		4. Pleased	
5. Angry		5. Surprised	
6. Helpless		6. Intrigued	
7. Guilty		7. Cheerful	
8. Stressed		8. Prideful	
9. Sad		9. Loving	
10. Disgusted		10. Joy	

Overall Positivity Score _____

Copyright © 2015 John Wiley and Sons, Inc. For use in Workbook only. Not to be reproduced without permission.

Chapter 4 Emotional Self-Control

Emotional Self-Control Defined

<u>Consciously moderating emotions</u>. Emotional self-control means intentionally managing your emotions and understanding how and when to demonstrate them appropriately. Emotionally intelligent leaders take responsibility for regulating their emotions and are not victims of them.

Using This Capacity

Appropriate use of this capacity changes depending on the setting and situation. However, we developed the following statements to provide a snapshot of what it *may* look like if someone is overusing or underusing this capacity. We then conducted focus groups with student leaders, and they vetted and added to the statements. A number of these statements are presented here.

Individuals who overuse this capacity may be perceived by others as:

- having difficulty in creating and maintaining healthy relationships;
- conceited, selfish, or so focused inwardly that others do not matter to them;
- overconfident in their abilities;
- unable or unwilling to change or try to do things differently;
- uptight and rigid.

Individuals who underuse this capacity may be perceived by others as:

- lacking a sense of what they do and don't do well;
- lacking follow-through;
- alienating others;
- having a difficult time developing a sense of team;
- lacking the skills and/or initiative to improve themselves;
- lacking self-awareness;
- unable to recognize and capitalize on strengths;
- untrustworthy.

Online Articles and Resources

- Consortium for Research on Emotional Intelligence in Organizations: www.eiconsortium.org
- Emotional intelligence information: www.unh.edu/emotional_intelligence
- Emotional Self-Control: Steps to Overcoming Reactive Patterns: www.helium.com
- How to Get Emotional Self-Control: Simply Speak Your Mind, Scientists Say: http://news.softpedia.com
- Internet directory on emotional intelligence: www.eq.org

- Personal website of scholar Reuven Bar-On: www.reuvenbaron .org
- Six Seconds: www.6seconds.org

Suggested Books

- *Becoming a Resonant Leader: Develop Your Emotional Intelligence, Renew Your Relationships, Sustain Your Effectiveness* by Richard E. Boyatzis, Fran Johnston, and Annie McKee
- *Building Emotional Intelligence: Techniques to Cultivate Inner Strength in Children* by Linda Lantieri and Daniel Goleman
- *Emotional Discipline: The Power to Choose How You Feel: Five Life Changing Steps to Feeling Better Every Day* by Charles Manz
- *Emotional Intelligence: Why It Can Matter More Than IQ* (10th anniv. ed.) by Daniel Goleman
- *Primal Leadership: Learning to Lead with Emotional Intelligence* by Daniel Goleman, Richard E. Boyatzis, and Annie McKee
- *Raising Your Emotional Intelligence: A Practical Guide* by Jeanne S. Segal
- *Working with Emotional Intelligence* by Daniel Goleman

Suggested Films

The following films highlight the capacity of emotional self-control. Some characters may overuse this capacity; others may lack the ability to use it successfully. As you watch any of the following, try and diagnose which characters are overusing or underusing this capacity, and who may be displaying an appropriate balance.

- *As Good as It Gets*
- *Avatar*
- *Billy Madison*

- *Captain Phillips*
- *The Chronicles of Narnia*
- *The Devil Wears Prada*
- *Finding Nemo*
- *Hancock*
- *Harold and Maude*
- *The Help*
- *Ice Age*
- *The Odd Couple*
- *Ordinary People*
- *Shrek*
- *Silver Linings Playbook*
- *Spider-Man*
- *Step Brothers*
- *Transformers*

Notable Quotes

I choose not to give energy to the emotions of revenge, hatred or the desire to subjugate.

    —*Rosanne Cash, singer*

_____

Any emotion, if it is sincere, is involuntary.

    —*Mark Twain, author*

_____

When dealing with people, remember you are not dealing with creatures of logic, but creatures of emotion.

    —*Dale Carnegie, author*

_____

Whether you win a match or lose a match, in terms of your emotions, it's important to be pretty levelheaded.

—*Maria Sharapova, tennis player*

———————

He liked to observe emotions; they were like red lanterns strung along the dark unknown of another's personality, marking vulnerable points.

—*Ayn Rand, author*

———————

My faith helps me overcome such negative emotions and find my equilibrium.

—*The Dalai Lama, spiritual leader*

Activity 4.1: Six Sources of Stress

Leadership is stressful. Emotionally intelligent leaders are acutely aware of the stressors in their environment. By naming them, a leader can better examine the situation and his or her response as well as determine how to manage a difficult situation.

Directions: Review the following sources of stress. Underline the sources that have affected you in the past 24 hours. Then, answer the reflection questions provided.

1. *Work Overload:* This source of stress occurs when there is too much to do in too little time. An example is a veteran on campus who has an internship or job, a full load of undergraduate classes, a daughter at home, and family obligations.

2. *Lack of Control:* When one does not have control over how time and energy is spent, lack of control becomes a source of stress. Similar to work overload, this stressor may be the result of pressing deadlines at work or a change in demands from an external force (e.g., school or work).

3. *Interaction Conflict:* Interaction conflict occurs when two (or more) individuals do not enjoy or get along with one another. This occurs in many different social settings including group projects in class, athletic teams, and student organizations.

4. *Issue Conflict:* Issue conflict occurs when there is a disagreement on how to address or navigate a challenge. On campus this may occur when some students want to eliminate hazing in their organization and others do not. Or, in student government, a faction may have an "issue" with the decision of those in power.

5. *Role Conflict:* Role conflict occurs where there is no clear delineation of who is responsible for a certain task or when two people have roles that are seemingly in conflict with one another. On campus, this may occur when a person feels another is "stepping on their toes" or taking over another person's role or task.

6. *Anticipatory Stressors:* Anticipatory stressors occur when a certain level of fear or anxiety exists about how something will turn out. A common example is the feeling a student may get before a speech or an exam. Managing conflict and working through differing perspectives or values may also cause anticipatory stress.

Source: Adapted from Whetten, D. A., & Cameron, K. S. (2010). *Developing management skills* (8th ed.). Upper Saddle River, NJ: Prentice Hall.

Copyright © 2015 John Wiley and Sons, Inc. For use in Workbook only. Not to be reproduced without permission.

What Do You Think?

- What were some of the most salient stressors for you?

- What does this activity tell you about your day-to-day workload?

- Why is it important to be aware of and name your default reactions to stress?

Copyright © 2015 John Wiley and Sons, Inc. For use in Workbook only. Not to be reproduced without permission.

Activity 4.2: **Three Reactions to Stress**

Reactions to stress are responses that we have to stressful situations. There is a wide range of behaviors within each of the following responses. Some behaviors are healthy, while others are destructive and dangerous. Emotionally intelligent leadership means being in tune with how you generally respond to stress and the ramifications for you and others.

Directions: Review the three reactions to stress listed below. In the blank space following each reaction, jot down your thoughts as to how this reaction may or may not relate to you, and, where applicable, provide examples.

1. *Aggression:* Aggression occurs when an individual assertively "attacks" the stressor. This may be as simple as aggressively completing a series of assignments or it could be a physical altercation with others. Being assertive and addressing stressors is necessary because leaders must work through difficult situations, but doing so in an appropriate manner is the key.

Copyright © 2015 John Wiley and Sons, Inc. For use in Workbook only. Not to be reproduced without permission.

2. *Repression:* Repression often involves ignoring or denying the stressor. The stressor may be so difficult to think about or address that it is repressed and largely ignored—even when logically, it should not be. This could be as simple as ignoring impending deadlines or exams, which can lead to larger issues, such as getting expelled from school or losing a leadership position in an organization. Repressing a stressor may be perfectly appropriate at times (e.g., no need to worry about finals in September), but eventually, it will need to be addressed and worked through.

3. *Fixation:* Almost the opposite of repression, fixation occurs when an individual intensely focuses on a stressor such as an exam, a big game, an assignment, or a disagreement with someone else. Some level of fixation can be healthy; however, taken to an extreme, it may become destructive to the individual and others. Similar to other reactions to stress, the appropriate level of fixation is the balance student leaders are looking to achieve, which is different for each person.

Source: Adapted from Whetten, D. A., & Cameron, K. S. (2010). *Developing management skills* (8th ed.). Upper Saddle River, NJ: Prentice Hall.

Copyright © 2015 John Wiley and Sons, Inc. For use in Workbook only. Not to be reproduced without permission.

Activity 4.3: Three Techniques for Managing Stress

Everyone has healthy and unhealthy ways to manage the stress they experience. For some, a long run will help, while others turn to food, alcohol, and other "quick fixes" to get them through stressful events. The following three techniques highlight healthy and unhealthy approaches to managing stress.

Directions: As you review the techniques listed, indicate which you most often demonstrate and identify how someone might see you managing stress.

1. *Reactive Strategies:* Reactive strategies are generally quick fixes that in isolation are not necessarily bad, but taken to an extreme are destructive to self and others. Examples of reactive strategies include drugs, alcohol, smoking, sex, food, shopping, gambling, television, and so on. Generally speaking, these techniques for managing stress are not healthy and will become another source of stress if abused.

2. *Proactive Strategies:* Proactive strategies generally build an individual's capacity to manage stress. Examples of proactive strategies may include: working out or exercise, a healthy diet, spirituality, therapy, relaxation, close relationships, and so on. By prioritizing proactive strategies, an individual becomes more resilient.

Copyright © 2015 John Wiley and Sons, Inc. For use in Workbook only. Not to be reproduced without permission.

3. *Enactive Strategies:* Employing an enactive strategy involves removing the stressor from your environment. If the stressor is a destructive member in your organization, perhaps you ask them to leave. If it is a problem with a roommate, perhaps you move out or choose not to room with them again next year. Of course, this approach can be taken to an extreme. No one can eliminate all stressors, and thus it is important to learn how to work with people through difficult situations.

Copyright © 2015 John Wiley and Sons, Inc. For use in Workbook only. Not to be reproduced without permission.

Activity 4.4: **Triggers**

Triggers are people, events, places, behaviors, and situations that make it difficult to maintain emotional self-control. Triggers are difficult to manage in real time, especially if we have not planned for them in advance. An understanding of your triggers will help you maintain emotional self-control in difficult situations so you can choose a response.

Directions: Spend some time brainstorming a short list of people, events, places, events, behaviors, and situations that trigger you. In addition, record how you react to the triggers (e.g., yelling, anger, shutting down).

People who trigger me: My reaction:
1.

2.

3.

4.

Places that trigger me: My reaction:
1.

2.

3.

4.

Events that trigger me: My reaction:
1.

2.

3.

4.

Copyright © 2015 John Wiley and Sons, Inc. For use in Workbook only. Not to be reproduced without permission.

Behaviors in others that trigger me:

My reaction:

1.

2.

3.

4.

Situations that trigger me:

My reaction:

1.

2.

3.

4.

Copyright © 2015 John Wiley and Sons, Inc. For use in Workbook only. Not to be reproduced without permission.

Activity 4.5: Choosing a Response

Directions: The objective of this activity is to brainstorm ways to successfully regulate emotions—techniques, tips, and tools for navigating triggers. In the numbered list below identify strategies for regulating emotions. Feel free to use smartphones, tablets, computers, or other resources to help compile your list. The goal is to identify techniques, tips, and tools throughout the course of the activity. Place a star next to ideas that you would like to investigate further.

Tips, Tools, and Techniques for Regulating Emotions

1.

2.

3.

4.

5.

6.

7.

8.

9.

10.

11.

12.

13.

14.

15.

Copyright © 2015 John Wiley and Sons, Inc. For use in Workbook only. Not to be reproduced without permission.

Activity 4.6: Emotional Self-Control in Presidential Politics

Directions: Watch C SPAN *Third 2008 Presidential Debate Full Video* on *YouTube*. While watching the video do your best to step outside of your personal feelings or political views. Debates are a challenging venue in which to maintain emotional self-control, and the objective of the task is to identify examples of effective emotional self-control and incidents of ineffective emotional self-control during the debate. In the table that follows record the nonverbal reactions, tone, or specific comments that demonstrate helpful and hurtful displays of emotion.

John McCain	Barack Obama
Helpful	Helpful
1.	1.
2.	2.
3.	3.
4.	4.
5.	5.
Hurtful	Hurtful
1.	1.
2.	2.
3.	3.
4.	4.
5.	5.

Copyright © 2015 John Wiley and Sons, Inc. For use in Workbook only. Not to be reproduced without permission.

Chapter 5   Authenticity

Activities

Authenticity Defined

<u>Being transparent and trustworthy</u>. Authenticity is about developing credibility, being transparent, and aligning words with actions. Emotionally intelligent leaders live their values and present themselves and their motives in an open and honest manner.

Using This Capacity

Appropriate use of this capacity changes depending on the setting and situation. However, we developed the following statements to provide a snapshot of what it *may* look like if someone is overusing or underusing this capacity. We then conducted focus groups with student leaders, and they vetted and added to the statements. A number of these statements are presented here.

Individuals who overuse this capacity may be perceived by others as:

• having difficulty in creating and maintaining healthy relationships;

- overly concerned with the thoughts and perceptions of others;
- self-righteous;
- unable to regulate thoughts and opinions that are best left unsaid;
- judgmental of others;
- above others.

Individuals who underuse this capacity may be perceived by others as:

- unable to be trusted;
- all talk and no action;
- needing to use authority or position power to get work done;
- valuing the end over the means;
- difficult to read or sending mixed signals.

Online Articles and Resources

- Authentic Leadership Development: www.hbs.edu/mba/academics/coursecatalog/2090.html
- Authentic Life: http://psych.athabascau.ca
- The Authentic Personality: http://personalpages.manchester.ac.uk
- Bill George: A Unique Life Story: http://youtube.com

Suggested Books

- *Authentic Leadership: Courage in Action* by Robert W. Terry
- *Authentic Leadership: Rediscovering the Secrets to Creating Lasting Value* by Bill George
- *Building an Authentic Leadership Image* by Center for Creative Leadership, Corey Criswell, and David P. Campbell
- *Courage: The Backbone of Leadership* by Gus Lee

- *Daring Greatly: How the Courage to Be Vulnerable Transforms the Way We Live, Love, Parent, and Lead* by Brené Brown
- *Finding Your True North: A Personal Guide* by Bill George, Andrew McLean, and Nick Craig
- *The Gifts of Imperfection: Let Go of Who You Think You're Supposed to Be and Embrace Who You Are* by Brené Brown
- *High Impact Leader: Moments Matter in Authentic Leadership Development* by Bruce Avolio and Fred Luthans
- *Jonathan Livingston Seagull* by Richard Bach
- *Leadership from the Inside Out: Becoming a Leader for Life* by Kevin Cashman
- *Let Your Life Speak* by Parker Palmer
- *Presence: Human Purpose and the Field of the Future* by Peter Senge, C. Otto Scharmer, Joseph Jaworski, and Betty Sue Flowers
- *Selfhood and Authenticity* by Corey Anton
- *True North: Discover Your Authentic Leadership* by Bill George, David Gergen, and Peter Sims

Suggested Films and Television Series

The following films and television shows highlight the capacity of authenticity. Some characters may overuse this capacity; others may lack the ability to use it successfully. As you watch any of the following, try and diagnose which characters are overusing or underusing this capacity, and who may be displaying an appropriate balance.

- *Billy Elliot*
- *Breaking Bad* (TV series)
- *Dead Poets Society*
- *The Devil Wears Prada*
- *Eat Pray Love*
- *Empire of the Sun*

- *Finding Forrester*
- *Good Will Hunting*
- *House of Cards* (TV series)
- *Pushing Hands*
- *Rain Man*
- *Shut Up and Sing*
- *Toy Story*
- *True Colors*
- *Whale Rider*

Notable Quotes

Honesty and transparency make you vulnerable. Be honest and transparent anyway.

—*Mother Teresa, founder of Missionaries of Charity*

It's hard to practice compassion when we're struggling with our authenticity or when our own worthiness is off-balance.

—*Brené Brown, educator and researcher*

We need to find the courage to say no to the things and people that are not serving us if we want to rediscover ourselves and live our lives with authenticity.

—*Barbara de Angelism, author*

I'm writing from a place of—a center of authenticity, somewhere that only I know how to write from.

—*K'naan, poet*

My work is about the establishment of trust. For someone to share their authenticity with me is a soul-to-soul thing. It's not a lens-to-soul thing.

—*Lisa Kristine, photographer*

_____

To find yourself, think for yourself.

—*Socrates, philosopher*

_____

The truth is the kindest thing we can give folks in the end.

—*Harriet Beecher Stowe, author*

Activity 5.1: Personal Core Values

Your personal core values help define who you are and what you care deeply about. They bring meaning to your life and guide behaviors and decisions.

Directions: From the sample core values below, check 6 to 8 values that resonate most with you. Feel free to add in additional values using the blank spaces.

☐ Achievement	☐ Growth	☐ Personal Development
☐ Adventure	☐ Hard Work	☐ Physical Challenge
☐ Arts	☐ Health	☐ Power
☐ Community	☐ Helping Others	☐ Recognition
☐ Competition	☐ Honesty/Integrity	☐ Respect
☐ Cooperation	☐ Inner Harmony	☐ Responsibility
☐ Courage	☐ Intellectual Stimulation	☐ Safety/Security
☐ Creativity	☐ Justice	☐ Service
☐ Democracy	☐ Kindness	☐ Spirituality
☐ Dependability	☐ Knowledge	☐ Stability
☐ Equality	☐ Leadership	☐ Status
☐ Excellence	☐ Love	☐ Sustainability
☐ Fairness	☐ Loyalty	☐ Truth
☐ Fame	☐ Nature	☐ Wealth
☐ Family	☐ Open Mindedness	☐ Wisdom
☐ Freedom	☐ Passion	☐ _____
☐ Friendship	☐ Peace	☐ _____

Copyright © 2015 John Wiley and Sons, Inc. For use in Workbook only. Not to be reproduced without permission.

Activity 5.2: Personal Core Values Prompts

Directions: Based on the values you identified in the *Personal Core Values* activity (5.1), discuss the following questions. As an alternative, you can record your responses if you are not working in a group.

• Which values do you think about frequently? How so?

• Which of these values do you find are *easy* to align with actions? Why do you think this is so?

• Which of these values do you find are *difficult* to align with actions? Why do you think this is so?

• Do any of these values conflict with each other? If so, how?

• What steps can you take to use your values to guide your actions in your life?

Copyright © 2015 John Wiley and Sons, Inc. For use in Workbook only. Not to be reproduced without permission.

Activity 5.3: **Personal Mission Statement**

A personal mission statement (also often called a personal credo, personal philosophy, or purpose statement) is a brief statement that identifies who you want to be and the principles by which you strive to live your life. A personal mission statement includes your core values and reflects your true purpose. Through this activity you will begin to construct your personal mission statement.

Part I

Directions: Respond to the following prompts. Do not overthink your responses. Rather, just brainstorm and write whatever comes to mind.

I am a person who . . .

I care deeply about . . .

My passions in life are . . .

Principles and values I want to live by are . . .

I want my life to be characterized by . . .

I enjoy spending my time . . .

The impact I want to have on others/on the world is . . .

I want to be remembered as someone who . . .

Copyright © 2015 John Wiley and Sons, Inc. For use in Workbook only. Not to be reproduced without permission.

Part II

Directions: Review your responses to the prompts in Part I and compile a two or three sentence mission statement that summarizes who you want to be and what you want to represent. You can begin by writing: My mission in life is . . . I strive to live my life . . . I am . . . My purpose . . . My life is . . .

Here is a sample personal mission statement:

I strive to live a life of balance, excellence, integrity, compassion, purpose, and service. I create positive change by building meaningful and mutual relationships, facilitating purposeful learning, promoting social justice, embracing sustainability, and striving for authenticity.

—*Paige Haber-Curran*

Draft of My Personal Mission Statement:

Copyright © 2015 John Wiley and Sons, Inc. For use in Workbook only. Not to be reproduced without permission.

Activity 5.4: Personal Mission Statement Action Planning

Directions: Record the personal mission statement you developed on the *Personal Mission Statement* activity (5.3) and answer the additional questions related to your personal mission statement.

My Personal Mission Statement:

Three things I should continue doing to live my mission:

Three things I can do to better live my mission:

People who can help hold me accountable to my mission:

I will remind myself of my Personal Mission Statement by . . .

Copyright © 2015 John Wiley and Sons, Inc. For use in Workbook only. Not to be reproduced without permission.

Chapter 6   Healthy Self-Esteem

Activities

6.1 This I Believe

6.2 Remember When

Healthy Self-Esteem Defined

<u>Having a balanced sense of self</u>. Healthy self-esteem is about balancing confidence in your abilities with humility. Emotionally intelligent leaders are resilient and remain confident when faced with setbacks and challenges.

Using This Capacity

Appropriate use of this capacity changes depending on the setting and situation. However, we developed the following statements to provide a snapshot of what it *may* look like if someone is overusing or underusing this capacity. We then conducted focus groups with student leaders, and they vetted and added to the statements. A number of these statements are presented here.

Individuals who overuse this capacity may be perceived by others as:

- arrogant, ignorant, or lacking concern for others;
- self-consumed;
- overconfident;
- unwilling to let others in.

Individuals who underuse this capacity may be perceived by others as:

- lacking confidence or belief in their abilities and/or ideas;
- uncomfortable making difficult decisions or speaking in front of a group;
- overcompensating and acting harsh or rigid;
- unwilling to tackle difficult challenges within the group;
- dispassionate;
- fragile.

Online Articles and Resources

- Different Kinds of Empathy: www.youtube.com/watch?v=eg2pq4Mjeyo
- Roy Baumeister, scholar: www.fsu.edu/profiles/baumeister
- Self-Esteem: The Costs and Causes of Low Self-Worth: www.jrf.org.uk
- The Trouble with Self-Esteem: www.nytimes.com
- A View on Buddhism: http://viewonbuddhism.org

Suggested Books

- *Attitudes, Beliefs and Choices* by Alexandra Delis-Abrams
- *Breaking the Chain of Low Self-Esteem* by Marilyn Sorensen
- *The Confidence Plan: How to Build a Stronger You* by Tim Ursiny
- *The Cultural Animal: Human Nature, Meaning, and Social Life* by Roy F. Baumeister
- *Self-Esteem: A Proven Program of Cognitive Techniques for Assessing, Improving, and Maintaining Your Self-Esteem* by Matthew McKay and Patrick Fanning
- *The Self-Esteem Companion: Simple Exercises to Help You Challenge Your Inner Critic and Celebrate Your Personal Strengths* by

Patrick Fanning, Carole Honeychurch, Catharine Sutker, and Matthew McKay

- *The Self-Esteem Workbook* by Glenn R. Schiraldi

Suggested Films

The following films highlight the capacity of healthy self-esteem. Some characters may overuse this capacity; others may lack the ability to use it successfully. As you watch any of the following, try and diagnose which characters are overusing or underusing this capacity, and who may be displaying an appropriate balance.

- *Apollo 13*
- *Billy Elliot*
- *Courage under Fire*
- *Dead Poets Society*
- *Erin Brockovich*
- *Finding Nemo*
- *The Full Monty*
- *Good Will Hunting*
- *Jonathan Livingston Seagull*
- *The King's Speech*
- *Kung Fu Panda*
- *Norma Rae*
- *Powder*
- *Pretty in Pink*
- *Ratatouille*
- *The Shawshank Redemption*
- *The Wizard of Oz*

Notable Quotes

You yourself, as much as anybody in the entire universe, deserve your love and affection.

   —*Siddhartha Gautama, founder of Buddhism*

_____

Never be bullied into silence. Never allow yourself to be made a victim. Accept no one's definition of your life; define yourself.

   —*Harvey Fierstein, actor and playwright*

_____

Every individual has a place to fill in the world, and is important, in some respect, whether he chooses to be so or not.

   —*Nathaniel Hawthorne, author*

_____

Self confidence is the first requisite to great undertakings.

   —*Dr. Samuel Johnson, author*

_____

If only you could sense how important you are to the lives of those you meet; how important you can be to people you may never even dream of. There is something of yourself that you leave at every meeting with another person.

   —*Fred Rogers, host of* Mr. Rogers' Neighborhood

_____

Disciplining yourself to do what you know is right and important, although difficult, is the high road to pride, self-esteem, and personal satisfaction.

   —*Margaret Thatcher, former prime minister of the United Kingdom*

_____

I really don't know how to be anyone else, and whenever I try to be anyone else, I fail miserably. Or I disappoint myself. It doesn't build my self-esteem, and it doesn't help me grow me at all.
　　—*Queen Latifah, entertainer*

I can be a rock star with a television show and still have a self-esteem problem. So it's nice to have your dad go, "Hey Melissa, I'm proud of you—you're doing good."
　　—*Melissa Etheridge, singer*

Never bend your head. Always hold it high. Look the world straight in the face.
　　—*Helen Keller, author*

Activity 6.1: **This I Believe**

Directions: This I Believe is an organization that encourages people to reflect "on the core values that guide their daily lives" (www.thisibelieve.org). By connecting with our core values that guide our lives we are able to build confidence in who we are and what we believe. Complete each sentence stem based on what you believe and what is most important to you.

A core belief I hold is . . . because . . .

I know that I am at my best when . . .

I love it when I . . .

Copyright © 2015 John Wiley and Sons, Inc. For use in Workbook only. Not to be reproduced without permission.

Activity 6.2: Remember When

Directions: An important factor that influences healthy self-esteem is how we feel about ourselves in connection to how others treat us. Think of a time when you were a part of a group that made you feel great just by being a member of the group. Write one or two sentences here that describe the group.

- What did the group do to make you feel like you belonged?

- How did you know that you belonged?

- What did you feel as a result of being part of this group?

- How would you describe your level of involvement with this group?

Copyright © 2015 John Wiley and Sons, Inc. For use in Workbook only. Not to be reproduced without permission.

Chapter 7   Flexibility

Flexibility Defined

Being open and adaptive to change. Flexibility is about adapting your approach and style based on changing circumstances. Emotionally intelligent leaders seek input and feedback from others and adjust accordingly.

Using This Capacity

Appropriate use of this capacity changes depending on the setting and situation. However, we developed the following statements to provide a snapshot of what it *may* look like if someone is overusing or underusing this capacity. We then conducted focus groups with student leaders, and they vetted and added to the statements. A number of these statements are presented here.

Individuals who overuse this capacity may be perceived by others as:

- arrogant, ignorant, or lacking concern for others;
- wishy-washy or indecisive;
- unwilling to take a stand;
- wanting to avoid confrontation;

- pushovers;
- lost in the possibilities.

Individuals who underuse this capacity may be perceived by others as:

- rigid or unyielding;
- unconcerned with the needs of others;
- being set in their ways;
- self-righteous;
- closed off to others' ideas.

Online Articles and Resources

- Foundations of Leadership III—Flexibility and Adaptability: http://ezinearticles.com/?Foundations-of-Leadership-III —Adaptability-and-Flexibility&id=1498415
- The Ken Blanchard Companies: www.kenblanchard.com
- Leadership and Flexibility: What We Can Learn from "The Elevator": www.fastcompany.com/blog
- Super Flexibility in Leadership: www.youtube.com
- The Versatile Leader: www.versatileleader.com

Suggested Books

- *Embracing Uncertainty: The Essence of Leadership* by Phillip G. Clampitt and Robert J. Dekoch
- *Leadership and the One Minute Manager: Increasing Effectiveness through Situational Leadership* by Ken Blanchard, Patricia Zigarmi, and Drea Zigarmi
- *Leading at a Higher Level: Blanchard on Leadership and Creating High Performing Organizations* by Ken Blanchard
- *Our Iceberg Is Melting: Changing and Succeeding under Any Conditions* by John Kotter and Holger Rathgeber
- *Primal Leadership: Learning to Lead with Emotional Intelligence* by Daniel Goleman, Richard E. Boyatzis, and Annie McKee

- *The Versatile Leader* by Bob Kaplan and Rob Kaiser
- *Who Moved My Cheese? An Amazing Way to Deal with Change in Your Work and in Your Life* by Spencer Johnson and Kenneth Blanchard

Suggested Films

The following films highlight the capacity of flexibility. Some characters may overuse this capacity; others may lack the ability to use it successfully. As you watch any of the following, try and diagnose which characters are overusing or underusing this capacity, and who may be displaying an appropriate balance.

- *Apollo 13*
- *The Candidate*
- *The Devil Wears Prada*
- *A Few Good Men*
- *Hancock*
- *Harry Potter* series
- *The Hunt for Red October*
- *The Last King of Scotland*
- *Miss Congeniality*
- *Pirates of the Caribbean* series
- *The Queen*
- *Shrek*
- *Spider-Man*
- *Thirteen Days*

Notable Quotes

Whatever is flexible and flowing will tend to grow, whatever is rigid and blocked will wither and die.

　　—*Tao Te Ching*

Empty your mind, be formless, shapeless—like water. Now you put water into a cup, it becomes the cup, you put water into a bottle, it becomes the bottle, you put it in a teapot, it becomes the teapot. Now water can flow or it can crash. Be water, my friend.
   —*Bruce Lee, actor*

Flexibility—in all aspects of life, the person with the most varied responses "wins."
   —*Kelly Perdew, author*

We're living in a different world now in terms of employee needs, and companies have to offer alternative methods for getting the work done. Even under the most difficult circumstances you can have creative flexibility.
   —*Anne M. Mulcahy, former chairperson and CEO of Xerox Corporation*

I am positive that flexibility is a feminine characteristic.
   —*Emma Bonino, Italian politician*

To make flexibility work, it is not only necessary to change our attitude about who is a good worker and who is not, but we have to train managers at all levels to recognize the difference between the number of hours worked and the quality of work produced.
   —*Madeleine M. Kunin, former governor of Vermont*

I like to think there are a lot of balls in the air, and the kids are not one that I choose to drop. They have been a priority and I have a career that allows for a little more flexibility at times and hours that are quite mom-friendly.

—*Elisabeth Hasselbeck, television personality*

Of course, running a coalition government in a country like India is a difficult task. More so when Congress leads the coalition, since most of the political parties were anti-Congress. To have a coalition, to run a coalition government, you require a lot of adjustments, a lot of flexibility.

—*Pranab Mukherjee, president of India*

Activity 7.1: Where Do You Stand on Change? Reflection Questions

Definition of Flexibility

Being open and adaptive to change. Flexibility is about adapting your approach and style based on changing circumstances. Emotionally intelligent leaders seek input and feedback from others and adjust accordingly.

Flexibility is a key capacity of emotionally intelligent leadership. Flexibility is a mindset (e.g., how you think about things and your preferences) and a skill set (e.g., your behaviors, actions, and abilities).

Directions: Respond to the prompts below about your experiences with the capacity of flexibility.

• How would you assess your overall flexibility mindset?

• What life experiences can you identify that have contributed to your flexibility mindset?

• What is one commitment you can make to yourself to further develop your flexibility mindset?

Copyright © 2015 John Wiley and Sons, Inc. For use in Workbook only. Not to be reproduced without permission.

- How would you assess your overall flexibility skill set?

- What life experiences can you identify that have contributed to your flexibility skill set?

- What is one commitment you can make to yourself to further develop your flexibility skill set?

If anything is certain, it is that change is certain. The world we are planning for today will not exist in this form tomorrow.

—*Philip Crosby*

Copyright © 2015 John Wiley and Sons, Inc. For use in Workbook only. Not to be reproduced without permission.

Activity 7.2: Innovation Station: Innovative Ideas

Note: This activity accompanies the *Innovation Station* module in the *Emotionally Intelligent Leadership for Students: Facilitation and Activity Guide.* See your facilitator for additional instructions.

Directions: For each round, write down the object your team was assigned and the innovative ideas your team generated for how the object can be used.

Round 1
   Assigned Object:

   Innovative Ideas Generated:

Round 2
   Assigned Object:

   Innovative Ideas Generated:

Copyright © 2015 John Wiley and Sons, Inc. For use in Workbook only. Not to be reproduced without permission.

Round 3
Assigned Object:

Innovative Ideas Generated:

Round 4
Assigned Object:

Innovative Ideas Generated:

Round 5
Assigned Object:

Innovative Ideas Generated:

Copyright © 2015 John Wiley and Sons, Inc. For use in Workbook only. Not to be reproduced without permission.

Activity 7.3: Innovation Station: Rating Your Experience

Note: This activity accompanies the *Innovation Station* module in the *Emotionally Intelligent Leadership for Students: Facilitation and Activity Guide*. See your facilitator for additional instructions.

Directions: On a scale of 1 (very poor) to 10 (excellent), how would you rate the following:

	Round 1	Round 2	Round 3	Round 4	Round 5
Team's performance					
Team's openness to ideas					
My openness to others' ideas					
Feeling that I was heard within the group					
How I feel about the overall experience					
My overall experience as being part of this team					

Copyright © 2015 John Wiley and Sons, Inc. For use in Workbook only. Not to be reproduced without permission.

Group discussion questions (to be completed after Round 4):

	Round 1 No Guidelines	Round 2 Critical and Skeptical	Round 3 Yes, and . . .	Round 4 Seeking to Understand
Pros				
Cons				

Copyright © 2015 John Wiley and Sons, Inc. For use in Workbook only. Not to be reproduced without permission.

Chapter 8   Optimism

Optimism Defined

<u>Having a positive outlook</u>. Optimism is about setting a positive tone for the future. Emotionally intelligent leaders use optimism to foster hope and generate energy.

Using This Capacity

Appropriate use of this capacity changes depending on the setting and situation. However, we developed the following statements to provide a snapshot of what it *may* look like if someone is overusing or underusing this capacity. We then conducted focus groups with student leaders, and they vetted and added to the statements. A number of these statements are presented here.

Individuals who overuse this capacity may be perceived by others as:

- out of touch with some of the challenges facing individuals in the group;
- overly excited for no apparent reason;
- not seeing the barriers inherent in the direction of the group;

- fake;
- annoyingly cheery;
- unaware of reality.

Individuals who underuse this capacity may be perceived by others as:

- having a difficult time establishing a positive tone;
- a drain on the energy of the group;
- negative and having a "glass half-empty" outlook;
- not open to possibilities and limited in their thinking;
- unable to see the positive in a situation;
- unable to inspire others to work at higher levels;
- a drag to be around;
- hopeless.

Online Articles and Resources

- The Happiness Formula: http://news.bbc.co.uk
- Inspire a Shared Vision: http://leadershipchallenge.typepad.com
- Muscle of Optimism: http://harvardmagazine.com
- Optimists Better at Regulating Stress: www.sciencedaily.com
- Seligman Touts the Art of Arguing with Yourself: www.apa.org
- This Is Your Brain on Optimism: www.newsweek.com/id/61572
- To Lead, Create a Shared Vision: http://hbr.harvardbusiness.org
- University of Pennsylvania, Positive Psychology Center: www.authentichappiness.sas.upenn.edu/Default.aspx

Suggested Books

- *Authentic Happiness: Using the New Positive Psychology to Realize Your Potential for Lasting Fulfillment* by Martin Seligman

- *Fish! A Proven Way to Boost Morale and Improve Results* by Stephen C. Lundin, Harry Pual, John Christensen, and Ken Blanchard
- *Happiness: Unlocking the Mysteries of Psychological Wealth* by Ed Diener and Robert Biswas-Diener
- *The High Impact Leader* by Bruce Avolio and Fred Luthans
- *Learned Optimism* by Martin Seligman
- *Optimism* by Helen Keller
- *Primal Leadership: Realizing the Power of Emotional Intelligence* by Daniel Goleman, Richard Boyatzis, and Annie McKee
- *Resonant Leadership* by Richard Boyatzis and Annie McKee
- *The Student Leadership Challenge* by James M. Kouzes and Barry Z. Posner

Suggested Films

The following films highlight the capacity of optimism. Some characters may overuse this capacity; others may lack the ability to use it successfully. As you watch any of the following, try and diagnose which characters are overusing or underusing this capacity, and who may be displaying an appropriate balance.

- *Anvil! The Story of Anvil*
- *Elf*
- *Finding Nemo*
- *Forrest Gump*
- *Groundhog Day*
- *Happy People*
- *It's a Wonderful Life*
- *Little Miss Sunshine*
- *Pleasantville*
- *Up*
- *Willy Wonka and the Chocolate Factory*

Notable Quotes

Optimism is the faith that leads to achievement. Nothing can be done without hope and confidence.

—*Helen Keller, author*

_____

One of the things I learned the hard way was that it doesn't pay to get discouraged. Keeping busy and making optimism a way of life can restore your faith in yourself.

—*Lucille Ball, actress*

_____

Truth is, I'll never know all there is to know about you just as you will never know all there is to know about me. Humans are by nature too complicated to be understood fully. So, we can choose either to approach our fellow human beings with suspicion or to approach them with an open mind, a dash of optimism and a great deal of candor.

—*Tom Hanks, actor*

_____

My optimism wears heavy boots and is loud.

—*Henry Rollins, artist*

_____

Comedy is acting out optimism.

—*Robin Williams, actor and comedian*

_____

There is a sense that things, if you keep positive and optimistic about what can be done, do work out.

—*Hillary Clinton, former U.S. Secretary of State*

_____

Habits of thinking need not be forever. One of the most significant findings in psychology in the last twenty years is that individuals can choose the way they think.

    —*Martin Seligman, author*

A leader is a dealer in hope.

    —*Napoleon Bonaparte*

Activity 8.1: Happy Networks?

Directions: In this activity you will examine optimism through the lens of social media. Using a social media site of your choice, examine the fifty most recent posts by others. Using the table that follows, tally the number of positive (e.g., I love this leadership class!), neutral (e.g., I ate corn for dinner.), and negative (e.g., I hate it when it rains.) comments or posts. Then, calculate percentages for each category.

Then, examine your own most recent twenty-five posts, tally the numbers, and determine the percentage of posts that are positive, benign, and negative.

Use the following key to complete your worksheet. Place a P, B, or N in the square.

P = Positive
B = Neutral
N = Negative

The fifty most recent posts by others on my social media site:

1.	2.	3.	4.	5.	6.	7.	8.	9.	10.
11.	12.	13.	14.	15.	16.	17.	18.	19.	20.
21.	22.	23.	24.	25.	26.	27.	28.	29.	30.
31.	32.	33.	34.	35.	36.	37.	38.	39.	40.
41.	42.	43.	44.	45.	46.	47.	48.	49.	50.

_____# of positive posts   _____% of positive posts

_____# of neutral posts   _____% of neutral posts

_____# of negative posts   _____% of negative posts

Copyright © 2015 John Wiley and Sons, Inc. For use in Workbook only. Not to be reproduced without permission.

My twenty-five most recent posts on my social media site:

1.	2.	3.	4.	5.	6.	7.	8.	9.	10.
11.	12.	13.	14.	15.	16.	17.	18.	19.	20.
21.	22.	23.	24.	25.					

_____# of positive posts   _____% of positive posts

_____# of neutral posts   _____% of neutral posts

_____# of negative posts   _____% of negative posts

Copyright © 2015 John Wiley and Sons, Inc. For use in Workbook only. Not to be reproduced without permission.

Activity 8.2: Optimism Scale

Directions: You will brainstorm behaviors of optimistic leadership and list them in the table that follows. After you have identified behaviors of optimistic leadership, assess two people you know (e.g., a classmate, boss, family member, friend). Place their names in the "Person 1" and "Person 2" columns in the table that follows and then assess them using the scale provided. Next, complete this assessment for yourself.

1 = Never   4 = Occasionally
2 = Very Rarely   5 = Frequently
3 = Rarely   6 = Very Frequently

Behaviors of Optimistic Leadership	Person 1	Person 2	You
1.			
2.			
3.			
4.			
5.			
6.			
7.			

Copyright © 2015 John Wiley and Sons, Inc. For use in Workbook only. Not to be reproduced without permission.

Behaviors of Optimistic Leadership	Person 1	Person 2	You
8.			
9.			
10.			
11.			
12.			
13.			
14.			
15.			

Copyright © 2015 John Wiley and Sons, Inc. For use in Workbook only. Not to be reproduced without permission.

Activity 8.3: Supportive Communication

Directions: Difficult conversations are challenging. Read each of the five strategies of supportive communication.

Circle two that, in general, are hard for you to use during difficult conversations with others (e.g., parents, siblings, friends, coworkers, group members, classmates).

Put a star by the behavior that you think will make the biggest difference in your leadership.

Supportive Communication Behaviors

1. *Communication is congruent, not incongruent.* Your verbal statements align with your nonverbal communication.

2. *Communication is problem oriented, not person oriented.* You focus on problems, behaviors, or issues and not the other person and his or her traits or characteristics.

3. *Communication is descriptive, not evaluative.* You describe an event, your reaction, then different courses of action.

4. *Communication is validating, not invalidating.* You communicate respect, and focus on areas of agreement in both what you say and how you say it.

5. *Listening.* You focus on truly hearing the other individual and focus on what is being said rather than what you are going to say next.

Source: Adapted from Whetten, D. A., & Cameron, K. S. (2010). *Developing management skills* (8th ed.). Upper Saddle River, NJ: Prentice Hall.

Copyright © 2015 John Wiley and Sons, Inc. For use in Workbook only. Not to be reproduced without permission.

Chapter 9   Initiative

Activities

Initiative Defined

<u>Taking action</u>. Initiative means being a self-starter and being motivated to take the first step. Emotionally intelligent leaders are ready to take action, demonstrate interest, and capitalize on opportunities.

Using This Capacity

Appropriate use of this capacity changes depending on the setting and situation. However, we developed the following statements to provide a snapshot of what it *may* look like if someone is overusing or underusing this capacity. We then conducted focus groups with student leaders, and they vetted and added to the statements. A number of these statements are presented here.

Individuals who overuse this capacity may be perceived by others as:

- off and running before others are up to speed;
- stepping over or using others to get what they want;

- too focused on the task and lacking focus on the process of building a team;
- leaving others behind;
- aggressive and putting self in front of others;
- competitive;
- unable to let others take the lead, unable to follow.

Individuals who underuse this capacity may be perceived by others as:

- lacking in their ability to inspire others;
- lacking direction;
- unable to set the tone for the organization;
- unable to put words and ideas into action;
- not taking their role seriously;
- not contributing to the team;
- a slacker or loafer.

Online Articles and Resources

- Find Your Passion: The Money Will Follow: http://womenentrepreneur.com
- Finding Your Passion: www.Entreprenuer.com
- Mihaly Csikszentmihalyi: Creativity, Fulfillment and Flow: www.youtube.com
- Solving Procrastination: An Application of Flow: www.kevinchiu.org

Suggested Books

- *Finding Flow: The Psychology of Engagement with Everyday Life* by Mihaly Csikszentmihalyi
- *Flow: The Psychology of Optimal Experience* by Mihaly Csikszentmihalyi

- *Girls Who Rocked the World: Heroines from Sacagawea to Sheryl Swoopes (Girls Know Best)* by Amelie Welden and Jerry McCann
- *Girls Who Rocked the World 2: From Harriet Tubman to Mia Hamm (v. 2)* by Michelle Roehm McCann, Jerry McCann, and Michelle Roehm
- *Hear Her Voice: Twelve Jewish Women Who Changed the World* by Miriam P. Feinberg and Miriam Klein Shapiro
- *No Opportunity Wasted: Creating a Life List* by Phil Keoghan and Warren Berger
- *Spiritual Leaders Who Changed the World: The Essential Handbook of the Past Century of Religion* by Ira Rifkin and Robert Coles
- *Women Who Changed the World* by Ros Horton and Sally Simmons

Suggested Films

The following films highlight the capacity of initiative. Some characters may overuse this capacity; others may lack the ability to use it successfully. As you watch any of the following, try and diagnose which characters are overusing or underusing this capacity, and who may be displaying an appropriate balance.

- *Apollo 13*
- *Avatar*
- *The Avengers*
- *Cast Away*
- *Chariots of Fire*
- *Charlie and the Chocolate Factory*
- *Election*
- *Finding Nemo*
- *Frozen*
- *Gattaca*

- *Hotel Rwanda*
- *The Incredibles*
- *Iron Jawed Angels*
- *Legally Blonde*
- *Little Mermaid*
- *March of the Penguins*
- *Miracle*
- *Patch Adams*
- *Rudy*
- *Saving Private Ryan*
- *Schindler's List*
- *The Shawshank Redemption*
- *Silkwood*

Notable Quotes

I would rather regret the things I have done than the things I have not.
   —*Lucille Ball, actress*

_____

Even if you're on the right track you'll get run over if you just sit there.
   —*Will Rogers, actor*

_____

If opportunity doesn't knock—build a door.
   —*Milton Berle, actor*

_____

The dynamic, creative present, however conditioned and restricted by the effects of prior presents, possesses genuine initiative.
   —*Corliss Lamont, philosopher*

_____

Time is neutral and does not change things. With courage and initiative, leaders change things.

—*Jesse Jackson, civil rights leader*

———————————

Success depends in a very large measure upon individual initiative and exertion, and cannot be achieved except by a dint of hard work.

—*Anna Pavlova, ballerina*

———————————

Hold up a mirror and ask yourself what you are capable of doing, and what you really care about. Then take the initiative—don't wait for someone else to ask you to act.

—*Sylvia Earle, oceanographer*

Activity 9.1: **Local Heroes**

Directions: This module is about honoring those who have made a difference at your school or in your local community. Your task is to research a local hero for whom you have great admiration. A few guidelines include:

- The person's contribution needs to be evident in either the school or community.
- The person may be living or deceased and should not be a friend or relative.
- The person may be a formal leader (elected official, coach, founder, teacher, etc.) or an informal leader (community member or activist) who took initiative to make the world a better place. This should be a person from your school or the local community.

Your research can be conducted in a number of ways: personal interview(s), online research, visiting the archives/library, speaking with a historian, and so on. Your biggest challenge will be a lack of time so you will need to be creative and take initiative.

Following are some criteria to guide your research:

- Name:

- Formal or informal leader:

- Major accomplishments:

- Challenges faced along the way:

- Personal attributes of the individual:

- How each of us benefits today because of their vision:

- Examples of how this person took initiative:

Copyright © 2015 John Wiley and Sons, Inc. For use in Workbook only. Not to be reproduced without permission.

Following are some reflection questions to consider upon completion:

- How did this individual display initiative to make a difference?

- What has been the lasting impact of the person's work and how do students benefit from their initiative?

- How does their work align with your own goals and aspirations?

Copyright © 2015 John Wiley and Sons, Inc. For use in Workbook only. Not to be reproduced without permission.

Record your findings in the space that follows.

Copyright © 2015 John Wiley and Sons, Inc. For use in Workbook only. Not to be reproduced without permission.

Activity 9.2: Four Reasons for Not Taking Action

Directions: Read the following passages and circle or underline key passages that you can personally relate to. Then, consider what you can do to overcome each barrier.

1. Fear of Failure

In each and every organization there are problems. Whether it is a team that hazes its new members, a community service group bogged down by decision making, or a new organization trying to grow its membership, effective leadership moves an organization past its challenges and unhealthy behaviors. The challenge is someone has to take the first step, and speaking out against the norm or going down an unknown path is risky. Thus, initiative takes courage because leadership can be dangerous. The thought of losing friends, looking foolish, or failing are enough to stop many leaders from taking initiative. There is an inherent danger in being first and taking initiative (e.g., if you are being hazed, are you willing to take a stand against it?). After all, a very public failure can occur if you attempt to influence the group to move in a certain direction and it doesn't. Fear of failing causes many people to stall, hold off, and ultimately choose a safer path. Emotionally intelligent leadership helps us take that first, difficult step.

2. Apathy

Another reason for inaction is the amount of work and energy it takes to begin the work. Many leaders simply do not have the energy to take on new efforts, and, as a result, problems persist. Every organization, group, and workplace has members who are apathetic, unmotivated, and lazy. However, when formal leaders are also apathetic and unmotivated, a dangerous and unhealthy dynamic occurs, and the organization, group, or workplace can quickly spiral downward. Tackling tough issues or starting something new takes a great deal of time and energy. Realizing this cost keeps many people from taking initiative.

Copyright © 2015 John Wiley and Sons, Inc. For use in Workbook only. Not to be reproduced without permission.

3. Popularity

A third reason for inaction is popularity. It may be deemed unpopular to take a stand against hazing and bullying, eating disorders, alcohol or drug abuse, counterproductive behavior, cheating, or other problems. The fear of being outcast by people we care about is a powerful force. As a result, many people go along with unhealthy practices, behaviors, and even personal habits. Each one of us have fallen victim to this because fitting in among peers is a major driver of behavior, no matter how old we are. We see this in athletics, politics, business, and other organizations. When was the last time you opted out of doing something different because you were afraid of what other people would think?

4. Managing Conflict

A final reason for not taking action is a fear of conflict. The desire to maintain harmony is a strong driver of behavior. This is especially true if you don't feel confident having difficult conversations or extended periods of conflict. This discomfort is a powerful influence on behavior and can keep us from acting. The fear of causing a problem or discussing the "elephant in the room" is too great. Of course, this fear exists in families, organizations, friendships, and groups. The downside of avoiding conflict is that problems persist, self-doubt may fester, and relationships and groups become divided. We all know what happens when a problem that isn't addressed escalates into something much bigger than it was initially. Taking action in the first place would have been a much better option.

Copyright © 2015 John Wiley and Sons, Inc. For use in Workbook only. Not to be reproduced without permission.

Activity 9.3: Solving Problems

The Five Steps of Problem Solving

When dealing with issues and problems we often encounter conceptual blocks that hold us back from making progress. Below are five steps that can be used to move past conceptual blocks. Highlight key phrases and ideas that will help you become a better problem solver.

1. *Determine roles.* Who will be leading the process, facilitating conversations, and ensuring you are staying on task? Who will keep time and keep notes or record minutes? What other roles might your group need to accomplish this task?

2. *Define the problem.* What exactly are you expected to accomplish? What is the ultimate objective or end product you are moving toward? Ensure that your problem is well defined. Otherwise, the remaining steps do not matter.

3. *Determine alternative solutions.* Brainstorm as many possibilities you can. The objective is to generate ten, twenty, thirty, forty-plus ideas. Do not pause and begin critiquing ideas—the goal at this stage is quantity not quality. Simply generate ideas.

4. *Decide on four to five ideas or options for further exploration.* Based on the different ideas generated in step 3, quickly identify the *four or five* most promising concepts and begin discussing the benefits and drawbacks of each.

5. *Do.* Choose your best idea or option based on the ultimate objective and execute.

Source: Adapted from Whetten, D. A., & Cameron, K. S. (2010). *Developing management skills* (8th ed.). Upper Saddle River, NJ: Prentice Hall.

Copyright © 2015 John Wiley and Sons, Inc. For use in Workbook only. Not to be reproduced without permission.

Chapter 10   Achievement

Activity
10.1 Getting to Flow

Achievement Defined

Striving for excellence. Achievement is about setting high personal standards and getting results. Emotionally intelligent leaders strive to improve and are motivated by an internal drive to succeed.

Using This Capacity

Appropriate use of this capacity changes depending on the setting and situation. However, we developed the following statements to provide a snapshot of what it *may* look like if someone is overusing or underusing this capacity. We then conducted focus groups with student leaders, and they vetted and added to the statements. A number of these statements are presented here.

Individuals who overuse this capacity may be perceived by others as:

- concerned only with the tasks at hand;
- not concerned with the people and relationships involved;
- too focused on winning and less concerned with how the group is winning;
- unethical and willing to bend the rules;

- impatient with others who are not moving as quickly;
- doing everything themselves;
- not making time for fun;
- difficult to please;
- overbearing;
- perfectionists.

Individuals who underuse this capacity may be perceived by others as:

- lacking direction;
- lazy or disinterested;
- disorganized;
- unable to follow through on commitments;
- always a follower, never a leader;
- unsuccessful.

Online Articles and Resources

- Dr. Wayne Dyer: The Power of Intention: www.youtube.com
- Locke's Goal Setting Theory—Understanding SMART Goal Setting: www.mindtools.com
- Motivation, Study Habits—Not IQ—Determine Growth in Math Achievement: www.sciencedaily.com
- Personal Goal Setting: www.mindtools.com
- Theory of Needs: www.12manage.com

Suggested Books

- *Art of Achievement: Mastering the Seven C's of Success in Business and Life* by Tom Morris
- *Finding Flow: The Psychology of Engagement with Everyday Life* by Mihaly Csikszentmihalyi

- *Finding Your Zone: Ten Core Lessons for Achieving Peak Performance in Sports and Life* by Michael Lardon and David Leadbetter
- *Flow: The Psychology of Optimal Experience* by Mihaly Csikszentmihalyi
- *How They Achieved: Stories of Personal Achievement and Business Success* by Lucinda Watson
- *The Magic of Thinking Big* by David Schwartz
- *NLP: The New Technology of Achievement* by NLP Comprehensive, Steve Andreas, and Charles Faulkner
- *The Power of Intention* by Wayne Dyer

Suggested Films

The following films highlight the capacity of achievement. Some characters may overuse this capacity; others may lack the ability to use it successfully. As you watch any of the following, try and diagnose which characters are overusing or underusing this capacity, and who may be displaying an appropriate balance.

- *Avatar*
- *Bend It Like Beckham*
- *The Devil Wears Prada*
- *The Hunger Games*
- *Invictus*
- *The Karate Kid*
- *Kung Fu Panda*
- *Legally Blonde*
- *Mad Hot Ballroom*
- *Miracle*
- *Rudy*
- *Searching for Bobby Fischer*
- *Slumdog Millionaire*

- *The Social Network*
- *Spellbound*
- *Star Trek* (2009)
- *Temple Grandin*
- *Up*

Notable Quotes

Trust yourself. Create the kind of self that you will be happy to live with all your life. Make the most of yourself by fanning the tiny, inner sparks of possibility into flames of achievement.

    —*Golda Meir, former prime minister of Israel*

You have to wonder at times what you're doing out there. Over the years, I've given myself a thousand reasons to keep running, but it always comes back to where it started. It comes down to self-satisfaction and a sense of achievement.

    —*Steve Prefontaine, runner*

Every successful individual knows that his or her achievement depends on a community of persons working together.

    —*Paul Ryan, U.S. representative*

With my academic achievement in high school I was accepted rather readily at Princeton and equally as fast at Yale, but my test scores were not comparable to that of my classmates. And that's been shown by statistics, there are reasons for that—there are cultural biases built into testing, and that was one of the motivations for the concept of affirmative action to try to balance out those effects.

—*Sonia Sotomayor, associate justice of the Supreme Court of the United States*

I want to say with the utmost of sincerity, not as a Republican, but as an American, that I have great respect for Senator Obama's historic achievement to become his party's nominee, not because of his color, but with indifference to it.

—*Mike Huckabee, former governor of Arkansas*

I think the fact that I made enough noise in the world that I might be remembered is an amazing achievement. You can't ask for more than that.

—*Nas, rapper*

Leaders are made, they are not born. They are made by hard effort, which is the price which all of us must pay to achieve any goal that is worthwhile.

—*Vince Lombardi, football coach, University of Notre Dame*

Activity 10.1: Getting to Flow

The concept of *flow* is important for understanding achievement. When we are in flow we are enthralled in the task at hand, we perform at very high levels, and we get a feeling of accomplishment through engaging in the task. This activity enables you to get insight from people who are close to you about when they have seen you at your best. This insight can help shed light on instances where you may have experienced flow.

Directions: First, you will watch the TEDTalk entitled *Flow: The Secret to Happiness*. Then, you will have 15 minutes to conduct five micro-interviews (1–2 minutes each) with people who know you well (parents, grandparents, coaches, mentors, coworkers, friends, etc.). These will be conducted via cell phone. Record your responses to the following questions.

Part 1

Interview 1

- Where have you seen me at my best?

- What activities was I engaged in?

- What goal did I achieve?

Copyright © 2015 John Wiley and Sons, Inc. For use in Workbook only. Not to be reproduced without permission.

Interview 2

- Where have you seen me at my best?

- What activities was I engaged in?

- What goal did I achieve?

Interview 3

- Where have you seen me at my best?

- What activities was I engaged in?

- What goal did I achieve?

Copyright © 2015 John Wiley and Sons, Inc. For use in Workbook only. Not to be reproduced without permission.

Interview 4

- Where have you seen me at my best?

- What activities was I engaged in?

- What goal did I achieve?

Part 2

Based on your research, develop a visual representation (e.g., drawing, picture) of what you heard.

Reference: Czikszentmihalyi, M. (2004, February). *Mihaly Csikszentmihalyi: Flow: The secret to happiness* [Video file]. www.ted.com/talks/mihaly_csikszentmihalyi_on_flow.html.

Copyright © 2015 John Wiley and Sons, Inc. For use in Workbook only. Not to be reproduced without permission.

Part 3

What Do You Think?

- What feedback surprised you?

- What feedback motivated you?

- How does the feedback you heard relate back to the capacity of achievement?

Copyright © 2015 John Wiley and Sons, Inc. For use in Workbook only. Not to be reproduced without permission.

Chapter 11   Consciousness of Others

Activities

Consciousness of Others Defined

Demonstrating emotionally intelligent leadership involves awareness of the abilities, emotions, and perceptions of others. Consciousness of others is about intentionally working with and influencing individuals and groups to effect positive change.

Online Articles and Resources

- Article on Followership: www.courageousfollower.net/articles -on-followership/
- Articles by Robert Cialdini: www.influenceatwork.com/articles/
- Barbara Kellerman on Bad Leadership: www.youtube.com /watch?v=_nRZWVTrTWM
- James MacGregor Burns on Leadership: www.youtube.com /watch?v=bugXWk820B8
- Leadership and Followership: What Tango Teaches Us about These Roles in Life: www.youtube.com/watch?v=Cswrnc1dggg
- Science of Persuasion: www.youtube.com/watch?v=cFdCzN7 RYbw

Suggested Books

- *Bad Leadership* by Barbara Kellerman
- *The Courageous Follower: Standing Up to and for Our Leaders* by Ira Chaleff
- *Influence: The Psychology of Persuasion* by Robert Cialdini
- *Leadership and the One Minute Manager: Increasing Effectiveness through Situational Leadership* by Ken Blanchard, Patricia Zigarmi, and Drea Zigarmi
- *Power of Followership* by Robert E. Kelley
- *Senior Leadership Teams: What It Takes to Make Them Great* by Ruth Wageman, Debra A. Nunes, James A. Burruss, and J. Richard Hackman

Suggested Films and Television Series

The following films and television shows highlight the facet of consciousness of others. Some characters may overuse this facet others may lack the ability to use it successfully. As you watch any of the following, try and diagnose which characters are overusing or underusing this facet, and who may be displaying an appropriate balance.

- *Billy Elliot*
- *The Birdcage*
- *The Color Purple*
- *Crash*
- *The Great Debaters*
- *Hoosiers*
- *Julie and Julia*
- *La Bamba*
- *Love Actually*

- *Milk*
- *Philadelphia*
- *The Pursuit of Happyness*
- *Remember the Titans*
- *Rudy*
- *Selena*
- *Strangers on a Train*
- *30 Rock (TV Show)*
- *12 Angry Men*

Notable Quotes

For beautiful eyes, look for the good in others; for beautiful lips, speak only words of kindness; and for poise, walk with the knowledge that you are never alone.

　　—Audrey Hepburn, actress

_____

Each person must live their life as a model for others.

　　—Rosa Parks, civil rights leader

_____

We simply attempt to be fearful when others are greedy and to be greedy only when others are fearful.

　　—Warren Buffett, investor

_____

Good actions give strength to ourselves and inspire good actions in others.

　　—Plato, ancient Greek philosopher

_____

It is not fair to ask of others what you are not willing to do yourself.

—*Eleanor Roosevelt, former first lady of the United States of America*

Consider the rights of others before your own feelings, and the feelings of others before your own rights.

—*John Wooden, basketball coach*

Vision is the art of seeing what is invisible to others.

—*Jonathan Swift, pamphleteer*

Although I don't have a prescription for what others should do, I know I have been very fortunate and feel a responsibility to give back to society in a very significant way.

—*Bill Gates, founder of Microsoft and philanthropist*

Activity 11.1: Discovering Individuals within a Group

Directions: You are tasked with filling in as many of the boxes as possible by gathering responses from other people. For each question find two people to answer the question. Your goal is to get responses from 20 different people. If you are not able to find 20 different people, you may gather more than one response from some people.

A role I like to play within a group is . . .	Name:	Name:
	Response:	Response:
A key strength I have when working in a group is . . .	Name:	Name:
	Response:	Response:
An area in which I would like to improve is . . .	Name:	Name:
	Response:	Response:
An adjective a friend would use to describe me when working in a group is . . .	Name:	Name:
	Response:	Response:
I feel alive when . . .	Name:	Name:
	Response:	Response:

Copyright © 2015 John Wiley and Sons, Inc. For use in Workbook only. Not to be reproduced without permission.

In a group I get irritated by . . .	Name:	Name:
	Response:	Response:
I am motivated by . . .	Name:	Name:
	Response:	Response:
I would describe my leadership style as . . .	Name:	Name:
	Response:	Response:
I am inspired by . . .	Name:	Name:
	Response:	Response:
People say I am good at . . .	Name:	Name:
	Response:	Response:

Copyright © 2015 John Wiley and Sons, Inc. For use in Workbook only. Not to be reproduced without permission.

Activity 11.2: **This Is Me . . .**

Note: This activity accompanies the *All Hands In* module in the *Emotionally Intelligent Leadership for Students: Facilitation and Activity Guide.* See your facilitator for additional instructions.

Directions: In each box jot down words, phrases, or pictures that reflect your responses to each prompt.

I am . . . (identities such as gender, race, age, etc.)	I would describe myself as . . . (characteristics, personality traits, personal qualities, etc.)
I care deeply about . . . (passions, values, issues, etc.)	I enjoy . . . (hobbies, activities, subjects in school, interests, etc.)

Copyright © 2015 John Wiley and Sons, Inc. For use in Workbook only. Not to be reproduced without permission.

Activity 11.3: **This Is We...**

Note: This activity accompanies the *All Hands In* module in the *Emotionally Intelligent Leadership for Students: Facilitation and Activity Guide.* See your facilitator for additional instructions.

Directions: In groups share your *This Is Me . . .* (*Student Workbook,* 11.2) responses and identify commonalities among the whole group, commonalities among smaller subgroups, and unique individual differences you may have.

Whole-Group Commonalities	Subgroup Commonalities

Individual Differences

Copyright © 2015 John Wiley and Sons, Inc. For use in Workbook only. Not to be reproduced without permission.

Chapter 12 Displaying Empathy

Displaying Empathy Defined

<u>Being emotionally in tune with others</u>. Empathy is about perceiving and addressing the emotions of others. Emotionally intelligent leaders place a high value on the feelings of others and respond to their emotional cues.

Using This Capacity

Appropriate use of this capacity changes depending on the setting and situation. However, we developed the following statements to provide a snapshot of what it *may* look like if someone is overusing or underusing this capacity. We then conducted focus groups with student leaders, and they vetted and added to the statements. A number of these statements are presented here.

Individuals who overuse this capacity may be perceived by others as:

- emphasizing people and their issues over process and productivity;
- unable to make difficult decisions;

- wasting too much time gaining consensus and buy-in from the group;
- unable to give people personal space;
- overly consumed in others' lives;
- lacking task orientation;
- overly accommodating;
- avoiding conflict.

Individuals who underuse this capacity may be perceived by others as:

- too focused on tasks;
- lacking the ability to connect with others;
- unable to connect with the group on a personal level;
- cold, aloof, or disinterested in others;
- not considering the human dynamic when making decisions;
- having difficulty in building meaningful relationships;
- self-absorbed.

Online Articles and Resources

- Beyond Video Games: Students Build Empathy Online: http://findarticles.com
- Brain Scans Show Children Naturally Prone to Empathy: http://newswise.com
- DEV Patnaik: http://cultureofempathy.com
- Empathy: The Human Connection to Patient Care: www.youtube.com/watch?v=cDDWvj_q-o8
- The Limits of Empathy: www.time.com
- President Barack Obama on Empathy: www.youtube.com/watch?v=LGHbbJ5xz3g
- Three Kinds of Empathy: Cognitive, Emotional, Compassionate: www.danielgoleman.info/blog
- What Your Employees Really Want: www.inc.com

Suggested Books

- *Creating Harmonious Relationships: A Practical Guide to the Power of True Empathy* by Andrew LeCompte
- *Empathy and Its Development* by Nancy Eisenberg and Janet Strayer
- *The Lost Art of Listening* by Michael P. Nichols
- *The Seven Habits of Highly Effective People* by Stephen R. Covey
- *Teaching Children Empathy, The Social Emotion: Lessons, Activities and Reproducible Worksheets (K–6) That Teach How to "Step into Others' Shoes"* by Tonia Caselman
- *A Way of Being* by Carl R. Rogers
- *Wired to Care: How Companies Prosper When They Create Widespread Empathy* by Dev Patnaik
- *Wisdom of Listening* by Mark Brady

Suggested Films

The following films highlight the capacity of displaying empathy. Some characters may overuse this capacity; others may lack the ability to use it successfully. As you watch any of the following, try and diagnose which characters are overusing or underusing this capacity, and who may be displaying an appropriate balance.

- *As It Is in Heaven*
- *Benny and Joon*
- *The Blind Side*
- *Dangerous Minds*
- *The Doctor*
- *The Fault in Our Stars*
- *Forrest Gump*
- *Hancock*
- *Ice Age* series

- *Lincoln*
- *My Sister's Keeper*
- *On the Waterfront*
- *To Kill a Mockingbird*
- *12 Angry Men*
- *Up in the Air*
- *What's Eating Gilbert Grape*

Notable Quotes

Most people do not listen with the intent to understand; they listen with the intent to reply. They're either speaking or preparing to speak. They're filtering everything through their own paradigms, reading their autobiography into other people's lives.
    —*Stephen R. Covey, author*

The struggle of my life created empathy—I could relate to pain, being abandoned, having people not love me.
    —*Oprah Winfrey, entertainer and philanthropist*

Traits like humility, courage, and empathy are easily overlooked—but it's immensely important to find them in your closest relationships.
    —*Laura Linney, actress*

Empathy is about standing in someone else's shoes, feeling with his or her heart, seeing with his or her eyes. Not only is empathy hard to outsource and automate, but it makes the world a better place.

—*Daniel H. Pink, author*

There's a gap somehow between empathy and activism. Rev. Dr. Martin Luther King, Jr. spoke of "soul force"—something that emanates from a deep truth inside of us and empowers us to act. Once you identify your inner genius, you will be able to take action, whether it's writing a check or digging a well.

—*Sue Monk Kidd, writer*

How far you go in life depends on you being tender with the young, compassionate with the aged, sympathetic with the striving and tolerant of the weak and the strong. Because someday in life you will have been all of these.

—*George Washington Carver, American educator and inventor*

To handle yourself, use your head; to handle others, use your heart.

—*Eleanor Roosevelt, former first lady and human rights leader*

Activity 12.1: Listening Probes

Note: This activity accompanies the *The Heart of Empathy: Listening* module in the *Emotionally Intelligent Leadership for Students: Facilitation and Activity Guide*. See your facilitator for additional instructions.

Directions: As you listen to each participant, pay close attention to which listening probes he or she is (or is not) using. Take notes so you can share your observations with the group.

Elaboration: Use when more information is needed (e.g., "Tell me more about . . .").

Clarification: Use when the message is unclear or ambiguous (e.g., "What do you mean by that?).

Repetition: Use when topic drift occurs or statements are unclear (e.g., "Once again, what do you think about . . . ?").

Reflection Probe: Use to encourage more in-depth pursuit of the same topic to ensure understanding (e.g., "So you are feeling uneasy about . . .").

Source: Adapted from Whetten, D. A., & Cameron, K. S. (2010). *Developing management skills* (8th Ed.). Upper Saddle River, NJ: Prentice Hall), p. 259.

Copyright © 2015 John Wiley and Sons, Inc. For use in Workbook only. Not to be reproduced without permission.

Activity 12.2: A Radical Experiment in Empathy

Directions: As you watch the TED video *Sam Richards: A Radical Experiment in Empathy,* answer the following questions and record additional observations as they come to mind.

- How does Sam Richards define empathy?

- What are examples from your own life that loosely align with Sam Richards' perspective?

- How does his message apply to leadership?

- Why is empathizing with others difficult to do sometimes?

- Can you think of a recent experience where you could have better empathized with another?

Additional Observations

Reference: Richards, S. (2011, April). *Sam Richards: A radical experiment in empathy* [Video file]. Retrieved from www.ted.com/talks/sam_richards_a_radical_experiment_in_empathy.html.

Copyright © 2015 John Wiley and Sons, Inc. For use in Workbook only. Not to be reproduced without permission.

Chapter 13   Inspiring Others

Activities

Inspiring Others Defined

<u>Energizing individuals and groups</u>. Inspiration occurs when people are excited about a better future. Emotionally intelligent leaders foster feelings of enthusiasm and commitment to organizational mission, vision, and goals.

Using This Capacity

Appropriate use of this capacity changes depending on the setting and situation. However, we developed the following statements to provide a snapshot of what it *may* look like if someone is overusing or underusing this capacity. We then conducted focus groups with student leaders, and they vetted and added to the statements. A number of these statements are presented here.

Individuals who overuse this capacity may be perceived by others as:

- too consumed with the future and vision;
- not in touch with the current realities "on the ground";

- lacking the ability to put vision into practice;
- unrealistic;
- lacking authenticity;
- being overly energetic.

Individuals who underuse this capacity may be perceived by others as:

- unable to get others excited about future directions;
- lacking a clear sense of purpose for self;
- being more concerned with the day-to-day versus the big picture;
- lacking energy and passion for a cause;
- unable to connect with others.

Online Articles and Resources

- American Rhetoric: www.americanrhetoric.com
- America's Best Leaders: http://content.ksg.harvard.edu
- Hartwick Leadership Institute: www.hartwickinstitute.org
- How to Inspire People Like Obama Does: www.businessweek .com
- The Time 100: www.time.com/time/time100/leaders/profile /king.html

Suggested Books

- *The Handbook of Emotionally Intelligent Leadership: Inspiring Others to Achieve Results* by Daniel A. Feldman
- *The Leader's Guide to Storytelling: Mastering the Art and Discipline of Business Narrative* by Stephen Denning
- *Leadership and Performance Beyond Expectations* by Bernard Bass
- *The Leadership Challenge* by James M. Kouzes and Barry Z. Posner
- *The Radical Leap* by Steve Farber

- *Resonant Leadership: Renewing Yourself and Connecting with Others through Mindfulness, Hope, and Compassion* by Richard E. Boyatzis and Annie McKee
- *The Secret Language of Leadership: How Leaders Inspire Action through Narrative* by Stephen Denning
- *Squirrel Inc.: A Fable of Leadership through Storytelling* by Stephen Denning

Suggested Films

The following films highlight the capacity of inspiring others. Some characters may overuse this capacity; others may lack the ability to use it successfully. As you watch any of the following, try and diagnose which characters are overusing or underusing this capacity, and who may be displaying an appropriate balance.

- *Apollo 13*
- *Braveheart*
- *Dead Poets Society*
- *Erin Brockovich*
- *Freedom Writers*
- *Friday Night Lights*
- *Glory*
- *The Hunger Games*
- *Iron Jawed Angels*
- *Jerry Maguire*
- *The Killing Fields*
- *Lean on Me*
- *Miracle*
- *Mona Lisa Smile*
- *Mr. Holland's Opus*
- *Pay It Forward*
- *Philadelphia*

- *Pitch Perfect*
- *Remember the Titans*
- *Rocky*
- *Rudy*

Notable Quotes

Our chief want is someone who will inspire us to be what we know we could be.

— *Ralph Waldo Emerson, poet*

Leaders establish the vision for the future and set the strategy for getting there; they cause change. They motivate and inspire others to go in the right direction and they, along with everyone else, sacrifice to get there.

— *John P. Kotter, author*

For a season, a gifted speaker can inspire with his words, but for a lifetime John McCain has inspired with his deeds.

— *Sarah Palin, former governor of Alaska*

I want to pay tribute to Diana myself. She was an exceptional and gifted human being. In good times and bad, she never lost her capacity to smile and laugh, nor to inspire others with her warmth and kindness. I admired and respected her—for her energy and commitment to others, and especially for her devotion to her two boys.

— *Queen Elizabeth II*

Transformational leaders behave in ways that motivate and inspire those around them by providing meaning and challenge to their followers' work. Team spirit is aroused. Enthusiasm and optimism are displayed. Leaders get followers involved in envisioning attractive future states; they create clearly communicated expectations that followers want to meet and also demonstrate commitment to goals and the shared vision.

—Bernard Bass, *leadership scholar*

Activity 13.1: **Everyday Inspiration**

!

Note: This activity accompanies the *Inspirational Items* module in the *Emotionally Intelligent Leadership for Students: Facilitation and Activity Guide.* See your facilitator for additional instructions.

   Directions: As you listen to people talk about what inspires them, record key words and phrases used when answering the following question: *Why is the item inspiring to you?*

Key Words	Key Phrases
1.	1.
2.	2.
3.	3.
4.	4.
5.	5.
6.	6.
7.	7.
8.	8.
9.	9.
10.	10.
11.	11.
12.	12.

Copyright © 2015 John Wiley and Sons, Inc. For use in Workbook only. Not to be reproduced without permission.

Three people in my life who most closely model the words and phrases above:

1.

2.

3.

What Do You Think?

- Inspiration is a pretty straightforward concept. Why is it so difficult to enact?

- How does this information help you connect the idea of inspiring others with leadership?

- What can you do to increase the capacity of inspiring others in yourself?

Copyright © 2015 John Wiley and Sons, Inc. For use in Workbook only. Not to be reproduced without permission.

Activity 13.2: Getting to Why

Directions: As you watch the video by Simon Sinek, answer the following question:

- Explain in your own words what Sinek means by the *what*.

- Explain in your own words what Sinek means by the *how*.

- Explain in your own words what Sinek means by the *why*.

Name five organizations that clearly and exceptionally communicate the *why*. If possible, identify videos or online resources that back up your assertion.

1.

2.

3.

4.

5.

Reference: Sinek, S. (2010, May 4). *Simon Sinek: How great leaders inspire action.* [Video file]. www.youtube .com/watch?v=qp0HIF3SfI4

Copyright © 2015 John Wiley and Sons, Inc. For use in Workbook only. Not to be reproduced without permission.

Activity 13.3: Mission Statements

Part 1

Directions: Read each of the mission statements listed below and place a star next to the two that you like the best. If you are in a group, circle the two mission statements that the group likes the best.

Amazon: "to be earth's most customer centric company; to build a place where people can come to find and discover anything they might want to buy online"

Apple: "bringing the best personal computing experience to students, educators, creative professionals and consumers around the world through its innovative hardware, software and Internet offerings"

Dell: "to be the most successful computer company in the world at delivering the best customer experience in markets we serve"

Facebook: "to give people the power to share and make the world more open and connected"

Google: "to organize the world's information and make it universally accessible and useful"

Microsoft: "to enable people and businesses throughout the world to realize their full potential"

Skype: "to be the fabric of real-time communication on the web"

Twitter: "a work in progress"

Yahoo!: "to be the most essential global Internet service for consumers and businesses"

YouTube: "to provide fast and easy video access and the ability to share videos frequently"

Reference: Hamilton, D. (2011, January 13). Top 10 company mission statements. http://drdianehamilton .wordpress.com/2011/01/13/top-10-company-mission-statements-in-2011/

Copyright © 2015 John Wiley and Sons, Inc. For use in Workbook only. Not to be reproduced without permission.

Part 2

Choose six of the mission statements and develop a well-crafted, succinct, and inspirational six-word statement that, in your mind, better communicates an inspirational mission.

Corporation	Six-Word Mission Statement
1.	
2.	
3.	
4.	
5.	
6.	

Copyright © 2015 John Wiley and Sons, Inc. For use in Workbook only. Not to be reproduced without permission.

Activity 13.4: Vision Statements

Part 1

Directions: Read each of the vision statements listed and place a star next to the two that you like the best. If you are in a group, circle the two vision statements that the group likes the best.

Allstate: "to reinvent protection and retirement for the consumer"

American Express: "the world's most respected service brand"

CVS: "to improve the quality of human life"

DuPont: "creating sustainable essentials to a better, safer and healthier life for people"

Harley-Davidson: "extraordinary motorcycles and customer experiences"

Hilton Worldwide: "to fill the earth with the light and warmth of hospitality"

Macy's: "a premier national retailer with iconic brands that each operate a multichannel business involving outstanding stores and dynamic online sites"

Reebok: "to help consumers, athletes and artists, partners and employees fulfill their true potential and reach heights they may have thought un-reachable"

Reference: McSween, D. (2010, December 4). Get inspiration from these 10 famous vision statements. www.brighthub.com/office/entrepreneurs/articles/98189.aspx

Copyright © 2015 John Wiley and Sons, Inc. For use in Workbook only. Not to be reproduced without permission.

Part 2

Choose six of the vision statements listed and develop a well-crafted, succinct, and inspirational six-word statement that in your mind better communicates an inspirational vision.

Corporation	Six-Word Vision Statement
1.	
2.	
3.	
4.	
5.	
6.	

Copyright © 2015 John Wiley and Sons, Inc. For use in Workbook only. Not to be reproduced without permission.

Chapter 14   Coaching Others

Coaching Others Defined

<u>Enhancing the skills and abilities of others.</u> Coaching is about helping others enhance their skills, talents, and abilities. Emotionally intelligent leaders know they cannot do everything themselves and create opportunities for others to develop.

Using This Capacity

Appropriate use of this capacity changes depending on the setting and situation. However, we developed the following statements to provide a snapshot of what it *may* look like if someone is overusing or underusing this capacity. We then conducted focus groups with student leaders, and they vetted and added to the statements. A number of these statements are presented here.

Individuals who overuse this capacity may be perceived by others as:

- too focused on developing others and not on other aspects of the organization;
- condescending;
- "holding people's hands";

- making others dependents versus building their capacity;
- too focused on others to focus on self or the larger purpose;
- treating others like children.

Individuals who underuse this capacity may be perceived by others as:

- lacking the ability to develop others on the team;
- disinterested in others on the team;
- hoarding information or power;
- self-centered;
- lacking trust in others' ability to perform.

Online Articles and Resources

- Center for Executive Coaching Blog: http://centerforexecutive coaching.com
- Coaching: The Fad That Won't Go Away: www.fastcompany .com/resources/learning/bolt/041006.html
- The Coaching Conundrum Report: www.blessingwhite.com
- Executive Coaching—Worth the Money?: http://blogs.wsj.com
- International Coach Federation: www.coachfederation.org
- Marshall Goldsmith: Ask the Coach: http://blogs.harvard business.org/goldsmith
- What an Executive Coach Can Do for You: http://hbswk.hbs .edu/archive/4853.html

Suggested Books

- *The Art and Practice of Leadership Coaching: Fifty Top Executive Coaches Reveal Their Secrets* by Howard Morgan, Phil Harkins, and Marshall Goldsmith
- *Coaching in Organizations: Best Coaching Practices from The Ken Blanchard Companies* by Madeleine Homan and Linda J. Miller

- *Coaching People: Expert Solutions to Everyday Challenges* by Harvard Business School Press
- *Coaching Questions: A Coach's Guide to Powerful Asking Skills* by Tony Stoltzfus
- *The Portable Coach: Twenty-Eight Surefire Strategies for Business and Personal Success* by Thomas Leonard
- *Reach for the Summit* by Pat Summitt
- *The Successful Coach: Insider Secrets to Becoming a Top Coach* by Terri Levine, Larina Kase, and Joe Vitale
- *They Call Me Coach* by John Wooden
- *Wooden on Leadership: How to Create a Winning Organization* by John Wooden

Suggested Films

The following films highlight the capacity of coaching others. Some characters may overuse this capacity; others may lack the ability to use it successfully. As you watch any of the following, try and diagnose which characters are overusing or underusing this capacity, and who may be displaying an appropriate balance.

- *Born into Brothels*
- *Bring It On*
- *Coach Carter*
- *Dead Poets Society*
- *Friday Night Lights*
- *Hoosiers*
- *The Karate Kid*
- *Lords of Dogtown*
- *Mad Hot Ballroom*
- *Million Dollar Baby*
- *Miracle*
- *Mona Lisa Smile*
- *Remember the Titans*

- *School of Rock*
- *Searching for Bobby Fischer*

Notable Quotes

I can cite numerous sponsors at different places in my career that made a huge difference for me just in terms of pulling me aside and giving me a tip or some coaching, or just watching what I was doing and not being afraid to tell me the truth about it.

—*Denise Morrison, president and chief executive officer of Campbell Soup Company*

A coach is someone who can give correction without causing resentment.

—*John Wooden, former UCLA basketball coach*

Our chief want in life is somebody who makes us do what we can.

—*Ralph Waldo Emerson, philosopher and poet*

Coaching is a profession of love. You can't coach people unless you love them.

—*Eddie Robinson, football coach, Grambling State University*

But with the right kind of coaching and determination you can accomplish anything and the biggest accomplishment that I feel I got from the film was overcoming that fear.

—*Reese Witherspoon, actress*

She taught me that it's OK to let down your guard and allow your players to get to know you. They don't care how much you know until they know how much you care.

—*Pat Summitt, former University of Tennessee women's basketball coach*

Activity 14.1: Listening Closely

Note: This activity accompanies the *Listening Closely* module in the *Emotionally Intelligent Leadership for Students: Facilitation and Activity Guide*. See your facilitator for additional instructions.

   Directions: When you are the observer, use the worksheet provided to document what you see and hear from the speaker. Capture key words or phrases that the speaker uses as well as any relevant factors (e.g., pace of speech, tone, volume).

Speaker's name:

Needs:

Interests:

Passions:

Concerns:

Hopes:

Emotions:

Other:

• What nonverbal demonstrations of effective listening did you notice?

Copyright © 2015 John Wiley and Sons, Inc. For use in Workbook only. Not to be reproduced without permission.

Activity 14.2: Setting Goals

Directions: Think about what skills, talents, and/or abilities you wish to improve in order to enhance your leadership capacity. List your response here:

There are two types of goals that can be useful when goal setting: SMART goals and stretch goals.

SMART Goals are more immediate and tangible goals. They are

S   specific
M   measurable
A   attainable
R   realistic
T   time bound

- What is one SMART goal that will help you improve your leadership capacity? (For example, "I will attend one workshop on public speaking by the end of this year.")

Stretch goals are goals that would make a significant difference in what you do, but you are not sure how you will accomplish them.

- What is one stretch goal that will help you improve your leadership capacity? (For example, "I will run for a leadership position in a club.")

Copyright © 2015 John Wiley and Sons, Inc. For use in Workbook only. Not to be reproduced without permission.

Chapter 15　Capitalizing on Difference

Activities
15.1 Wheel of Difference
15.2 Strength or Challenge?

Capitalizing on Difference Defined

<u>Benefiting from multiple perspectives</u>. Capitalizing on difference means recognizing our unique identities, perspectives, and experiences are assets, not barriers. Emotionally intelligent leaders appreciate and use difference as an opportunity to create a broader perspective.

Using This Capacity

Appropriate use of this capacity changes depending on the setting and situation. However, we developed the following statements to provide a snapshot of what it *may* look like if someone is overusing or underusing this capacity. We then conducted focus groups with student leaders, and they vetted and added to the statements. A number of these statements are presented here.

Individuals who overuse this capacity may be perceived by others as:

- too focused on accommodating everyone;
- too focused on the process and not on getting results;

- seeking out difference rather than ability or talent;
- excluding people from dominant social identity groups.

Individuals who underuse this capacity may be perceived by others as:

- missing opportunities to widen the perspective of the organization;
- narrow in focus;
- unable or unwilling to see differing viewpoints;
- only surrounding themselves with people who are similar to them;
- afraid of difference or change.

Online Articles or Resources

- Capitalizing on Diversity: www.businessweek.com
- Capitalizing on Diversity: Interpersonal Congruence in Small Work-Groups: www.hbs.edu
- Companies Capitalizing on Worker Diversity: www.nytimes.com
- In Students' Eyes, Look-Alike Lawyers Don't Make the Grade: www.nytimes.com
- Racial Equity: www.wkkf.org
- Resources for Cultural Diversity at Work: www.diversitycentral.com/diversity_store/search.php
- White Privilege by Peggy McIntosh: www.nymbp.org/reference/WhitePrivilege.pdf

Suggested Books

- *The Difference: How the Power of Diversity Creates Better Groups, Firms, Schools, and Societies* by Scott E. Page
- *Five Regions of the Future: Preparing Your Business for Tomorrow's Technology Revolution* by Joel Arthur Barker and Scott Erickson

- *Harvard Business Review on Managing Diversity* by R. Roosevelt Thomas, David A. Thomas, Robin J. Ely, and Debra Meyerson
- *Making Diversity Work: Seven Steps for Defeating Bias in the Workplace* by Sondra Thiederman
- *Paradigms: The Business of Discovering the Future* by Joel Arthur Barker
- *Play to Your Strengths: Stacking the Deck to Achieve Spectacular Results for Yourself and Others* by Andrea Sigetich and Carol Leavitt
- *Putting Our Differences to Work: The Fastest Way to Innovation, Leadership, and High Performance* by Debbe Kennedy and Joel A. Barker
- *Strengths-Based Leadership* by Tom Rath and Barry Conchie

Suggested Films

The following films highlight the capacity of capitalizing on difference. Some characters may overuse this capacity; others may lack the ability to use it successfully. As you watch any of the following, try and diagnose which characters are overusing or underusing this capacity, and who may be displaying an appropriate balance.

- *Avatar*
- *The Blind Side*
- *Crash*
- *Dallas Buyers Club*
- *Fantastic Four*
- *Glory*
- *Glory Road*
- *Harry Potter* series
- *Lord of the Rings* trilogy
- *Milk*
- *Miracle*

- *Ocean's 11*
- *Ocean's 12*
- *Remember the Titans*
- *Star Wars* series
- *Toy Story 3*
- *Traffic*
- *X-Men*

Notable Quotes

We all live with the objective of being happy; our lives are all different and yet the same.

—*Anne Frank, author*

_____

Differences challenge assumptions.

—*Anne Wilson Schaef, author*

_____

For those who have seen the Earth from space, and for the hundreds and perhaps thousands more who will, the experience most certainly changes your perspective. The things that we share in our world are far more valuable than those which divide us.

—*Donald Williams, astronaut*

_____

As long as the differences and diversities of mankind exist, democracy must allow for compromise, for accommodation, and for the recognition of differences.

—*Eugene McCarthy, former U.S. senator*

_____

In a politically diverse nation, only by finding that common ground can we achieve results for the common good.

    —*Olympia Snowe, former U.S. senator*

We have become not a melting pot but a beautiful mosaic. Different people, different beliefs, different yearnings, different hopes, different dreams.

    —*Jimmy Carter, thirty-ninth president of the United States*

If we are to achieve a richer culture, rich in contrasting values, we must recognize the whole gamut of human potentialities, and so weave a less arbitrary social fabric, one in which each diverse human gift will find a fitting place.

    —*Margaret Mead, cultural anthropologist*

Activity 15.1: **Wheel of Difference**

A person's identity can be comprised of four realms: core, social identities, other identities, and experience.

Directions: Review the figure below and the different realms of identity described. Additional directions follow.

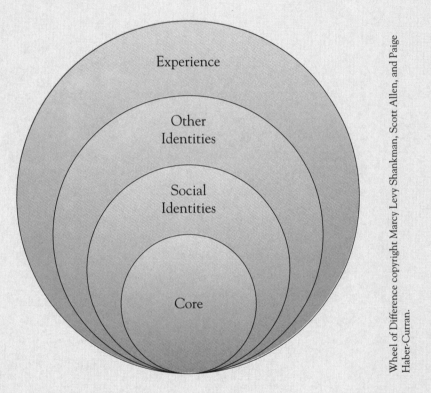

Wheel of Difference copyright Marcy Levy Shankman, Scott Allen, and Paige Haber-Curran.

Realm	Elements
Your core	Personality, beliefs, values
Your social identities	Gender identity, race, ethnicity, age, ability, sexual orientation, socioeconomic status
Other identities	Marital status, geographic location, religion, nationality, income, family status, physical appearance, upbringing
Experience	Education, knowledge, employment level, work experience, field of employment, leisure activities, personal habits

Copyright © 2015 John Wiley and Sons, Inc. For use in Workbook only. Not to be reproduced without permission.

1. Review the elements in the wheel and circle six to eight elements that mean the most to you.
2. Place a star by the three or four elements that you are most conscious of on a daily basis.
3. In the following space, jot your thoughts about what stands out to you from this activity.

Copyright © 2015 John Wiley and Sons, Inc. For use in Workbook only. Not to be reproduced without permission.

Activity 15.2: **Strength or Challenge?**

Directions: One's strengths can benefit a group by positively contributing to the group and its process and purpose. On the other hand, depending on the context or whether the strength is taken to an extreme, a strength can become a weakness.

First, write in the My Strengths column, the skills, talents, or areas of knowledge that you often bring to groups to which you belong. Then, in the next column identify the contributions that each strength can bring to a group. Last, in the third column identify challenges that each strength can bring if taken to an extreme or not utilized well.

My Strength	Contribution	Challenge

Copyright © 2015 John Wiley and Sons, Inc. For use in Workbook only. Not to be reproduced without permission.

Chapter 16 Developing Relationships

Developing Relationships Defined

<u>Building a network of trusting relationships</u>. Developing relationships means creating meaningful connections. Emotionally intelligent leaders encourage opportunities for relationships to grow and develop.

Using This Capacity

Appropriate use of this capacity changes depending on the setting and situation. However, we developed the following statements to provide a snapshot of what it *may* look like if someone is overusing or underusing this capacity. We then conducted focus groups with student leaders, and they vetted and added to the statements. A number of these statements are presented here.

Individuals who overuse this capacity may be perceived by others as:

- losing sight of the tasks that need to be accomplished in the organization;
- playing favorites with people with whom they "click";

- fake or superficial if there are not authentic motives behind their actions;
- annoying.

Individuals who underuse this capacity may be perceived by others as:

- unable to connect on a personal level with others;
- uncaring or self-centered;
- uninterested in others;
- too focused on tasks and outcomes rather than people or process;
- lacking trust.

Online Articles and Resources

- *Harvard Business Review*—How Leaders Create and Use Networks: http://hbr.org/product/how-leaders-create-and-use-networks/an/R0701C-PDF-ENG
- LinkedIn Labs (inmaps): http://inmaps.linkedinlabs.com
- Skills That Make Us a Good Partner Make Us a Good Parent: www.sciencedaily.com
- Ten Tips for Successful Business Networking: www.business knowhow.com/tips/networking

Suggested Books

- *Becoming a Resonant Leader: Develop Your Emotional Intelligence, Renew Your Relationships, Sustain Your Effectiveness* by Richard E. Boyatzis, Fran Johnston, and Annie McKee
- *Exploring Leadership: For College Students Who Want to Make a Difference* by Susan R. Komives, Nance Lucas, and Timothy McMahon
- *The Leadership Challenge* by James M. Kouzes and Barry Z. Posner

- *Transformational Leadership* by Bernard M. Bass and Ronald E. Riggio
- *Transforming Leadership* by James MacGregor Burns
- *Whale Done! The Power of Positive Relationships* by Kenneth Blanchard, Thad Lacinak, Chuck Tompkins, and Jim Ballard

Suggested Films

The following films highlight the capacity of developing relationships. Some characters may overuse this capacity; others may lack the ability to use it successfully. As you watch any of the following, try and diagnose which characters are overusing or underusing this capacity, and who may be displaying an appropriate balance.

- *Avatar*
- *Beaches*
- *The Breakfast Club*
- *Dead Man Walking*
- *The Descendents*
- *Divine Secrets of the Ya-Ya Sisterhood*
- *Forrest Gump*
- *Fried Green Tomatoes*
- *Good Will Hunting*
- *The Karate Kid*
- *Mean Girls*
- *Midnight in Paris*
- *Miracle*
- *Powder*
- *Rudy*
- *The Shawshank Redemption*
- *The Sisterhood of the Traveling Pants*
- *Sleepless in Seattle*
- *Terms of Endearment*

- *Up*
- *Up in the Air*

Notable Quotes

Whenever you're in conflict with someone, there is one factor that can make the difference between damaging your relationship and deepening it. That factor is attitude.
    —*William James, psychologist and philosopher*

Friendship is born at that moment when one person says to another, "What! You too? I thought I was the only one."
    —*C. S. Lewis, author*

Developing a relationship with someone you admire, who can encourage you to reach your full potential, is something that everyone can benefit from.
    —*Mandy Moore, singer and actress*

Through my research, I found that vulnerability is the glue that holds relationships together. It's the magic sauce.
    —*Brene Brown, educator*

All I can say is the most important part of being in a relationship is that you love the person for who they are.
    —*Liv Tyler, actress*

Activity 16.1: Active Listening Overview

Active listening is a vital skill for relationship building. The following behaviors contribute to effective active listening.

    Directions: Review the behaviors of active listening below. Place a check mark next to the behaviors that you often use when others are speaking, and place an X next to the behaviors that you do not use very often when others are speaking.

- Be attentive.

- Seek to understand.

- Show interest.

- Engage your nonverbals (e.g., nodding, leaning in, smiling, eye contact).

- Try to recognize emotions behind the words.

- Paraphrase and reflect back what is being said.

- Ask questions or for clarification to better understand.

- Allow speaker to complete his or her thoughts without interrupting him or her.

- Show respect.

- Be open to what the person is saying.

Copyright © 2015 John Wiley and Sons, Inc. For use in Workbook only. Not to be reproduced without permission.

Activity 16.2: Personal Networking Web

Networking is an essential tool for building relationships. This activity helps you identify different constituents who are in your personal network.

Directions: Write your name in the circle. Brainstorm different constituents in your life (e.g., professors, classmates, teachers, immediate and extended family, advisors, alumni and alumnae, roommates, teammates, friends of the family, coaches, organizations) and write their names in the blank space on the paper. Then, by drawing lines, connect each name you wrote down to your name and to other names when there is a direct connection between the constituents. Additionally, you may add people with whom you do not have a direct connection but who have a direct connection to one of your constituents by connecting them using dashed lines. Do not spend too much time wondering whether someone should be on your web or not; if someone comes to mind go ahead and add them to your web.

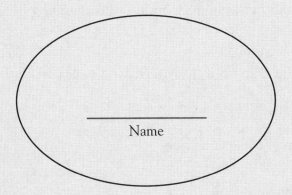

Name

Copyright © 2015 John Wiley and Sons, Inc. For use in Workbook only. Not to be reproduced without permission.

Activity 16.3: Personal Networking Action Planning

Directions: Refer to your web from the *Personal Networking Web* activity (16.2) and answer the following questions.

- What patterns do you see in your personal networking web? Do you see any gaps?

- Who in your personal networking web do you see as particularly important for helping you connect you to other people?

- What opportunities do you see in your personal network web that you can utilize in the next three months?

- What potential connections can you facilitate for a friend or classmate?

- What connections or relationships may require some additional attention or reconnection to maintain this relationship in the future?

- How do you see your personal networking web changing in the next three years?

- What steps can you take right now to expand your personal networking web?

Other thoughts regarding your web:

Copyright © 2015 John Wiley and Sons, Inc. For use in Workbook only. Not to be reproduced without permission.

Chapter 17   Building Teams

Building Teams Defined

<u>Working with others to accomplish a shared purpose</u>. Building teams is about effectively communicating, creating a shared purpose, and clarifying roles to get results. Emotionally intelligent leaders foster group cohesion and develop a sense of "we."

Using This Capacity

Appropriate use of this capacity changes depending on the setting and situation. However, we developed the following statements to provide a snapshot of what it *may* look like if someone is overusing or underusing this capacity. We then conducted focus groups with student leaders, and they vetted and added to the statements. A number of these statements are presented here.

Individuals who overuse this capacity may be perceived by others as:

- too focused on team and not focused on other aspects of the organization;
- creating an atmosphere of group think;
- relying too much on others to get things done;

- unable to take personal responsibility or initiative because they are too focused on the team.

Individuals who underuse this capacity may be perceived by others as:

- unable to inspire a group of people toward a common purpose;
- doing everything themselves;
- minimizing the contributions of others;
- not valuing other members of the group;
- unable to trust or consider the ideas of others.

Online Articles or Resources

- Belbin Team Roles: An Introduction: www.youtube.com
- Belbin Team Role Theory: www.belbin.com
- Belbin Team Roles Training Bite: www.youtube.com
- Bruce Tuckman's Forming, Storming, Norming, Performing Model: www.businessballs.com
- Simulation Training Systems: www.stsintl.com/index.html
- Surprising Pitfalls of Teamwork Training: www.businessweek.com
- Wilderdom: www.wilderdom.com/games

Suggested Books

- *The Five Dysfunctions of a Team: A Leadership Fable* by Patrick Lencioni
- *Groups That Work (and Those That Don't): Creating Conditions for Effective Teamwork* by J. Richard Hackman
- *Leading Teams: Setting the Stage for Great Performances* by J. Richard Hackman
- *Overcoming the Five Dysfunctions of a Team* by Patrick Lencioni
- *The Seventeen Essential Qualities of a Team Player: Becoming the Kind of Person Every Team Wants* by John C. Maxwell

- *Team of Rivals* by Doris Kearns Goodwin
- *When Teams Work Best: 6,000 Team Members and Leaders Tell What It Takes to Succeed* by Frank M. J. LaFasto and Carl E. Larson
- *The Wisdom of Teams: Creating a High Performance Organization* by Jon R. Katzenbach and Douglas K. Smith

Suggested Films and Television Series

The following films and television shows highlight the capacity of building teams. Some characters may overuse this capacity; others may lack the ability to use it successfully. As you watch any of the following, try and diagnose which characters are overusing or underusing this capacity, and who may be displaying an appropriate balance.

- *Any Given Sunday*
- *The Blind Side*
- *Bring It On*
- *Eight Men Out*
- *Facing the Giants*
- *The Great Debaters*
- *Grey's Anatomy* (TV series)
- *Hoosiers*
- *A League of Their Own*
- *Major League*
- *Miracle*
- *Ocean's 11*
- *The Office* (TV series)
- *Pitch Perfect*
- *Remember the Titans*
- *Rudy*
- *Star Trek into Darkness*
- *White Squall*

Notable Quotes

Trust lies at the heart of a functioning, cohesive team. Without it, teamwork is all but impossible.

—*Patrick Lencioni, author*

I've got a great staff and great support system, and I'm going to stick my neck out and do what I always do.

—*Pat Summitt, former University of Tennessee women's basketball coach*

By choosing the team path instead of the working group, people commit to take the risks of conflict, joint work-products, and collective action necessary to build a common purpose, set of goals, approach, and mutual accountability.

—*Jon R. Katzenbach and Douglas K. Smith, authors*

I tell people in their careers, "Look for growth. Look for the teams that are growing quickly. Look for the companies that are doing well. Look for a place where you feel that you can have a lot of impact."

—*Sheryl Sandberg, chief operating officer of Facebook*

Activity 17.1: Egg Drop Self- and Team Assessment

Note: This activity accompanies the *Egg Drop Challenge* module in the *Emotionally Intelligent Leadership for Students: Facilitation and Activity Guide.* See your facilitator for additional instructions.

Part 1: Assessment of the Team

Directions: Assess your **team** during the activity based on the following criteria:

	Poor	Adequate	Good	Excellent
Overall performance				
Positive environment to share ideas				
Investment of team members in the goal				
Having a common vision				
Effective communication				
Everyone was valued as part of the team				
Different perspectives and ideas were sought out				

- What our team did well was . . .

- What our team could improve on was . . .

Copyright © 2015 John Wiley and Sons, Inc. For use in Workbook only. Not to be reproduced without permission.

Part 2: Assessment of Self

Directions: Assess **yourself** during the activity based on the following criteria:

	Poor	Adequate	Good	Excellent
My contributions to the team				
My investment in the process				
My ability to listen to other teammates				
My communication skills				
Seeking out different ideas and perspectives				

- Ways in which I contributed to the team's process were . . .

- Areas in which I could have improved as a teammate were . . .

Copyright © 2015 John Wiley and Sons, Inc. For use in Workbook only. Not to be reproduced without permission.

Activity 17.2: **Building Teams:** *Remember the Titans*

Directions: Review Tuckman's Stages of Group Development provided in the table that follows. Then, watch the *Remember the Titans* movie clip and identify examples from the movie that reflect the different stages of the model.

If you have access to the *Remember the Titans* DVD, watch the movie from 10:30 to 43:00. If you do not, use these movie clips from the Internet:

Creation of a Team Pt. 1 (*Remember the Titans*) www.youtube.com/watch?v=6M 6pAh-HhMc (10 minutes)

Creation of a Team Pt. 2 (*Remember the Titans*) www.youtube.com/watch?v=sgK -_r_nnkc (10 minutes)

Tuckman's Stages of Group Development	Example from *Remember the Titans*
Forming: The team is formed. People are getting to know each other, and the team begins agreeing on goals and determining how to work together.	
Storming: Differing ideas or perspectives are voiced, which can cause tension or friction within a group. At this stage emotions tend to run high, and conflicts can arise. The group must figure out how to work through this. Some groups get stuck in this stage, while others progress.	

Copyright © 2015 John Wiley and Sons, Inc. For use in Workbook only. Not to be reproduced without permission.

Tuckman's Stages of Group Development	Example from *Remember the Titans*
Norming: The team comes together and focuses on a common goal. Behavioral norms (acceptable ways of behaving) are agreed upon, and some members let go of their own ideas and personal goals in order to help the team function. Through this, team members become more committed and take responsibility for the team and their role in the team.	
Performing: The team is able to work effectively together and can tackle new goals or challenges, come to consensus, and create results.	

Reference: Tuckman, B. (1965). Developmental sequence in small groups. *Psychological Bulletin, 63*(6), 384–399.

Copyright © 2015 John Wiley and Sons, Inc. For use in Workbook only. Not to be reproduced without permission.

Chapter 18   Demonstrating Citizenship

Activities

Demonstrating Citizenship Defined

<u>Fulfilling responsibilities to the group</u>. Citizenship is about being actively engaged and following through on your commitments. Emotionally intelligent leaders meet their ethical and moral obligations for the benefit of others and the larger purpose.

Using This Capacity

Appropriate use of this capacity changes depending on the setting and situation. However, we developed the following statements to provide a snapshot of what it *may* look like if someone is overusing or underusing this capacity. We then conducted focus groups with student leaders, and they vetted and added to the statements. A number of these statements are presented here.

Individuals who overuse this capacity may be perceived by others as:

- dogmatic or overly focused on the rules;
- having overly unrealistic expectations of people;

- lacking empathy for individual situations;
- lacking flexibility in response to changing circumstances;
- overly passionate about issues.

Individuals who underuse this capacity may be perceived by others as:

- struggling to model the way;
- not living up to well established norms and expectations;
- unable to give up part of themselves for the benefit of the whole;
- not truly committed to the group—just themselves;
- selfish or stubborn;
- lacking concern for society or issues larger than themselves.

Online Articles and Resources

- Citizenship: http://plato.stanford.edu/entries/citizenship/
- *Citizenship, Democracy and Ethnocultural Diversity Newsletter:* www.queensu.ca/cded/news.html
- *Citizenship Studies—an Academic Journal:* www.tandf.co.uk
- Justice with Michael Sandel: www.justiceharvard.org

Suggested Books

- *A Brief History of Citizenship* by Derek Heater
- *Citizenship: A Very Short Introduction* by Richard Bellamy
- *Citizenship Papers: Essays* by Wendell Berry
- *Good Business* by Mihaly Csikszentmihalyi
- *Preparing for Citizenship: Teaching Youth to Live Democratically* by Ralph L. Mosher, Robert A. Kenny Jr., and Andrew Garrod
- *The Quickening of America: Rebuilding Our Nation, Remaking Our Lives* by Frances Moore Lappé and Paul Martin DuBois
- *The Remains of the Day* by Kazuro Ishiguro
- *The Spirit of Community: The Reinvention of American Society* by Amitai Etzioni

- *Take Action! A Guide to Active Citizenship* by Marc Kielburger and Craig Kielburger
- *What Is Citizenship?* by Derek Heater

Suggested Films and Television Series

The following films and television shows highlight the capacity of demonstrating citizenship. Some characters may overuse this capacity; others may lack the ability to use it successfully. As you watch any of the following, try and diagnose which characters are overusing or underusing this capacity, and who may be displaying an appropriate balance.

- *Abraham Lincoln* (A&E biography)
- *Argo*
- *The Butler*
- *Dalai Lama* (A&E biography)
- *Eleanor Roosevelt* (A&E biography)
- *Erin Brockovich*
- *Frederick Douglass* (A&E biography)
- *Hancock*
- *Hoot*
- *Iron Jawed Angels*
- *Milton Hershey* (A&E biography)
- *Nelson Mandela* (A&E biography)
- *The New Heroes* (PBS series)
- *Remember the Titans*
- *To Kill a Mockingbird*

Notable Quotes

It is not always the same thing to be a good man and a good citizen.
—*Aristotle, ancient Greek philosopher*

Good government is no substitute for self-government.
    —*Mohandas Gandhi, leader of the Indian Nationalist Movement*

―――――――――

We must stop thinking of the individual and start thinking about what is best for society.
    —*Hillary Clinton, former U.S. secretary of state*

―――――――――

A nation, as a society, forms a moral person, and every member of it is personally responsible for his society.
    —*Thomas Jefferson, third president of the United States*

―――――――――

The efforts of the government alone will never be enough. In the end the people must choose and the people must help themselves.
    —*John F. Kennedy, thirty-fifth president of the United States*

―――――――――

As a citizen, you need to know how to be a part of it, how to express yourself—and not just by voting.
    —*Sandra Day O'Connor, former associate justice of the Supreme Court of the United States*

Activity 18.1: Key Aspects of Effective Followership

Directions: Review the five qualities and behaviors of effective followers that follow (Kelley, 1995). Then, using this framework, answer the reflection questions.

1. Effective followers are committed to the organization and its purpose.
2. Effective followers work hard and have high standards of performance.
3. Effective followers act in line with the values and mission of the organization.
4. Effective followers are credible.
5. Effective followers are dependable.

What Do You Think?

- Do you agree with these characteristics? Why? Why not?

- Which characteristics did you see exemplified in the video *Leadership from a Dancing Guy?* (see References for video link)

- Which characteristics do you see as crucial within an organization? Briefly explain.

- Which characteristics are lacking in your own organizations? How might you improve this reality?

References: Kelley, R. E. (1995). In praise of followers. In J. T. Wren (Ed.), *The leader's companion* (pp. 193–204). New York, NY: Free Press.

Leadership from a Dancing Guy [Video].www.youtube.com/watch?v=hO8MwBZl-Vc or http://vimeo.com/30386180#

Copyright © 2015 John Wiley and Sons, Inc. For use in Workbook only. Not to be reproduced without permission.

Activity 18.2: Acts of Citizenship

Directions: The following behaviors could be considered acts of citizenship. Consider each of the behaviors, assessing each along the three criteria of (1) amount of effort, (2) amount of time, and (3) level of importance. Rate from 1 to 10, with 1 = very low and 10 = very high. }}

	Amount of Effort (1–10)	Amount of Time (1–10)	Importance (1–10)
Voting in a student government election			
Attending student organization meetings			
Confronting a peer who is not following through on his or her responsibilities			
Meeting deadlines when you volunteer			
Educating yourself on current issues affecting your campus			
Helping someone who looks to be in need			
Contacting a facilities worker if an automatic accessible door for disabled persons is not functioning			
Not using the automatic accessible door for disabled persons in order to help extend the working life of the door			
Mentoring a student who is struggling			
Standing up for someone who is not being heard			
Organizing a petition to create change on campus			

Copyright © 2015 John Wiley and Sons, Inc. For use in Workbook only. Not to be reproduced without permission.

	Amount of Effort (1–10)	Amount of Time (1–10)	Importance (1–10)
Running for a leadership role in a campus organization to effect change			
Providing suggestions to improve a program on campus			
Completing a campus climate or student experience survey for your campus			
Volunteering your time in the community			
Planning an event to address a campus need			

- What other acts of citizenship can you identify on your campus?

Copyright © 2015 John Wiley and Sons, Inc. For use in Workbook only. Not to be reproduced without permission.

Activity 18.3: Committing to Citizenship

Directions: Refer to the *Acts of Citizenship* activity (18.2). Review the acts of citizenship and identify two or three ways you can commit to increasing your level of citizenship on campus. Additionally, identify the time frame in which this will take place (e.g., next executive board meeting or next semester).

Commitment   Time Frame

1.

2.

3.

Copyright © 2015 John Wiley and Sons, Inc. For use in Workbook only. Not to be reproduced without permission.

Activity 18.4: Citizenship-Driven Organization

Directions: Imagine a student organization in which everyone is actively engaged and a contributing member of the group. What would that ideal organization look like? Design a student organization that encourages and enables group citizenship of all members using the prompts that follow.

Organization's Name:

Organization's Purpose:

Organizational Structure (e.g., leadership roles, any groups/ committees, or other structures):

Description of specified roles within the organization (if applicable):

Expectations and guidelines for group membership:

How will group members be recruited and introduced/oriented into the organization?

Other ideas:

Copyright © 2015 John Wiley and Sons, Inc. For use in Workbook only. Not to be reproduced without permission.

Chapter 19   Managing Conflict

Managing Conflict Defined

<u>Identifying and resolving conflict</u>. Managing conflict is about working through differences to facilitate the group process. Emotionally intelligent leaders skillfully and confidently address conflicts to find the best solution.

Using This Capacity

Appropriate use of this capacity changes depending on the setting and situation. However, we developed the following statements to provide a snapshot of what it *may* look like if someone is overusing or underusing this capacity. We then conducted focus groups with student leaders, and they vetted and added to the statements. A number of these statements are presented here.

Individuals who overuse this capacity may be perceived by others as:

- stalling progress to please everyone;
- unrealistic in their desire for everyone to get along;
- overly focused on group process;

- overanalyzing group dynamics and conflict;
- seeking out conflict to manage when it may not be there or may not be important or relevant;
- "stirring the pot."

Individuals who underuse this capacity may be perceived by others as:

- letting problems fester within the group;
- unable to take a stand when needed;
- spineless or lacking confidence;
- holding the group back because of their inability to address underlying issues;
- passive aggressive;
- lacking commitment to the group or trust within the group.

Online Articles and Resources

- Center for Conflict Dynamics Hot Buttons: www.conflict dynamics.org/products/cdp/hb/
- Choosing a Conflict Management Style: http://disputere solution.ohio.gov
- Leadership Development: Conflict Management for College Student Leaders: www.mediate.com/articles/rashidJ1.cfm
- Program on Negotiation at Harvard Law School Clearinghouse: www.pon.org/catalog/index.php
- Thomas-Kilmann Conflict MODE Instrument: www.kilmann .com/conflict.html

Suggested Books

- *Beyond Reason: Using Emotions as You Negotiate* by Roger Fisher and Daniel Shapiro
- *Conflict Management: Resolving Disagreements in the Workplace* (3rd ed., Crisp Fifty-Minute Books) by Herbert S. Kindler

- *The Coward's Guide to Conflict: Empowering Solutions for Those Who Would Rather Run Than Fight* by Tim Ursiny
- *Difficult Conversations: How to Discuss What Matters Most* by Douglas Stone, Bruce Patton, Sheila Heen, and Roger Fisher
- *Fierce Conversations: Achieving Success at Work and in Life, One Conversation at a Time* by Susan Scott
- *Getting to Yes* by Bruce M. Patton, William L. Ury, and Roger Fisher
- *Managing Conflict with Your Boss* by Center for Creative Leadership, Davida Sharpe, and Elinor Johnson

Suggested Films and Television Series

The following films and television shows highlight the capacity of managing conflict. Some characters may overuse this capacity; others may lack the ability to use it successfully. As you watch any of the following, try and diagnose which characters are overusing or underusing this capacity, and who may be displaying an appropriate balance.

- *Abraham Lincoln* (A&E biography)
- *Bring It On*
- *Gandhi*
- *Glory*
- *Harry Potter* series
- *Hotel Rwanda*
- *Major League*
- *Metallica: Some Kind of Monster*
- *Nelson Mandela* (A&E biography)
- *Ralph Bunche: An American Odyssey*
- *Schindler's List*
- *1776*
- *Thirteen Days*
- *12 Angry Men*

- *12 Years a Slave*
- *Up in the Air*
- *War of the Roses*

Notable Quotes

You gain strength, courage and confidence by every experience in which you must stop and look fear in the face.

—*Eleanor Roosevelt, former first lady of the United States*

Never in this world can hatred be stilled by hatred; it will be stilled only by non-hatred; this is the law eternal.

—*Siddhartha Gautama, founder of Buddhism*

People on both sides of any conflict believe they are right, whether it's on a TV show or in the real world.

—*Mandy Patinkin, actor and singer*

This conflict is one thing I've been waiting for. I'm well and strong and young—young enough to go to the front. If I can't be a soldier, I'll help soldiers.

—*Clara Barton, educator, nurse, and humanitarian*

Work on developing a cooperative relationship, so when conflict comes, you believe you are allies.

—*Dean Tjosvold, director of the Hong Kong Cooperative Learning Center*

Smooth seas do not make skillful sailors.
  —*African proverb*

Out beyond ideas of rightdoing and wrongdoing, there is a field. I will meet you there.
  —*Rumi, poet and philosopher*

Everything that irritates us about others can lead us to an understanding of ourselves.
  —*Carl Jung, psychologist*

Activity 19.1: Five Approaches to Managing Conflict

Directions: Below are five ways in which conflict can be managed. Review the five approaches. Underline any words or phrases that stand out to you. Then, rank how you prefer to manage conflict, from 1 (engage in this approach most often) to 5 (engage in this approach least often).

_____ *Competing:* You are assertive and stand up for what you believe is the best solution. You know how to defend your position and will do so to get your way.

_____ *Collaborating:* You strike a balance between being assertive and being cooperative. You attempt to create a "win-win" situation.

_____ *Compromising:* You give a little to get a little. This means you look to find the best solution for all as quickly and easily as possible.

Copyright © 2015 John Wiley and Sons, Inc. For use in Workbook only. Not to be reproduced without permission.

_____   *Avoiding:* You are willing to give in or give up before a conflict starts. This may mean you postpone addressing the issue or you simply withdraw from the situation.

_____   *Accommodating:* You sacrifice what you want to help the situation get resolved. You put the other person's needs ahead of your own and work to find a solution to satisfy that person more than yourself.

Now that you've ranked these approaches to conflict, reflect on these five ways of managing conflict, write notes about when you have engaged in each and how well you think you did in those situations.

Reference: Adapted from Thomas, K. W., & Kilmann, R. H. (2007). *Thomas-Kilmann conflict mode instrument.* Mountain View, CA: CPP, Inc.

Copyright © 2015 John Wiley and Sons, Inc. For use in Workbook only. Not to be reproduced without permission.

Activity 19.2: **Commitment to Act**

Learning how to manage conflict is more than just thinking about when you have been in a conflict situation. It's also about deciding how you will approach and handle future conflicts.

Directions: Think of three people with whom you have experienced conflict in the past. Then, consider the following prompts and finish each statement. Be sure to identify specific and actionable behaviors that you can put into practice. It may be helpful to review the *Five Approaches to Managing Conflict* activity (19.1).

The next time I experience conflict with _____
Name

I will . . .

The next time I experience conflict with _____
Name

I will . . .

The next time I experience conflict with _____
Name

I will . . .

Copyright © 2015 John Wiley and Sons, Inc. For use in Workbook only. Not to be reproduced without permission.

Activity 19.3: Sources of Conflict

Directions: Listed below are eight common sources of conflict. Can you identify these sources of conflict in your own experiences? Jot down notes about who the conflict was with and what the conflict entailed in the space provided below each source of conflict.

Eight Common Sources of Conflict

1. *Conflicting Needs:* Limited resources (like money, attention from others, or supplies)

2. *Conflicting Styles:* Personality differences, approaches to tasks or work styles

3. *Conflicting Perceptions:* Individual experiences and perspectives

4. *Conflicting Goals:* Differences in what needs to be accomplished or how success is defined

Copyright © 2015 John Wiley and Sons, Inc. For use in Workbook only. Not to be reproduced without permission.

5. *Conflicting Pressures*: Differing roles and responsibilities mean differing levels of pressure

6. *Conflicting Roles*: What is expected of each person, formally or informally

7. *Conflicting Values*: What matters to each of us and what we each consider "right"

8. *Inconsistent Policies*: Accepted rules of behavior are frequently changed or inconsistently applied

Reference: Adapted from Bell, A. (2002). Six ways to resolve workplace conflicts. McLaren School of Business, University of San Francisco. www.usfca.edu/fac-staff/bell/article15.html;

Hart, B. (2000). Conflict in the workplace. Behavioral Consultants, P.C. www.excelatlife.com/articles /conflict_at_work.htm

Copyright © 2015 John Wiley and Sons, Inc. For use in Workbook only. Not to be reproduced without permission.

Activity 19.4: Pieces of the Pie

Directions: After reviewing the *Sources of Conflict* activity (19.3), draw a pie chart that reflects the sources of conflict in your life today. Each source of conflict will comprise a slice of pie. The size of each pie slice should reflect the relevance of the conflict in your life—the larger the piece, the more relevant or salient the conflict.

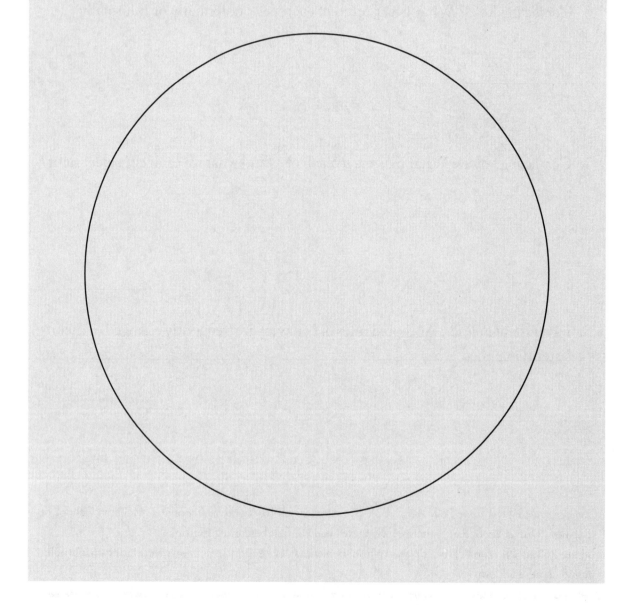

Copyright © 2015 John Wiley and Sons, Inc. For use in Workbook only. Not to be reproduced without permission.

Refer to your pie and consider the following questions:

- Where do you see the most conflict in your life? What does this mean to you?

- How much difficulty does each source of conflict cause you?

- Which sources of conflict are the most manageable? Least?

- If each source of conflict could be resolved, what difference would this make in your life?

Copyright © 2015 John Wiley and Sons, Inc. For use in Workbook only. Not to be reproduced without permission.

Chapter 20   Facilitating Change

Activities

20.1 Roles of Change Agents

20.2 Levels of Resistance

20.3 Resistance Can Be Good

Facilitating Change Defined

<u>Working toward new directions.</u> Facilitating change is about advancing ideas and initiatives through innovation and creativity. Emotionally intelligent leaders seek to improve on the status quo and mobilize others toward a better future.

Using This Capacity

Appropriate use of this capacity changes depending on the setting and situation. However, we developed the following statements to provide a snapshot of what it *may* look like if someone is overusing or underusing this capacity. We then conducted focus groups with student leaders, and they vetted and added to the statements. A number of these statements are presented here.

Individuals who overuse this capacity may be perceived by others as:

- creating busy work for the organization;
- never satisfied, relentless, and pushing too hard;

- always looking ahead and unable to enjoy or celebrate accomplishments;
- challenging the group at a rate that's difficult to absorb;
- impatient.

Individuals who underuse this capacity may be perceived by others as:

- satisfied with the status quo;
- unable to help the organization navigate new challenges or directions;
- lacking influence or initiative;
- missing opportunities for growth and development of the group;
- apathetic.

Online Articles and Resources

- Change Management: http://changingminds.org
- Change Management blog: www.change-management-blog.com
- Leading Change blog: www.fastcompany.com
- Leading Change: A Model by John P. Kotter: www.esi-intl.com
- Leading Change: Creating an Organization That Lives Change: www.Inc.com
- Personal website of John Kotter: www.johnkotter.com

Suggested Books

- *All Hat and No Cattle: Shaking Up the System and Making a Difference at Work* by Chris Turner
- *The Dance of Change: The Challenges to Sustaining Momentum in Learning Organizations* by Peter M. Senge, Art Kleiner, Charlotte Roberts, and George Roth
- *The Heart of Change: Real-Life Stories of How People Change Their Organizations* by John P. Kotter and Dan S. Cohen

- *Immunity to Change: How to Overcome It and Unlock the Potential in Yourself and Your Organization* by Robert Kegan and Lisa Laskow Lahey
- *Leadership for a Better World: Understanding the Social Change Model of Leadership Development* by Susan R. Komives and Wendy Wagner
- *Leading Change* by John P. Kotter
- *Managing Change and Transition* by Richard Luecke and Harvard Business School Press
- *Managing Transitions: Making the Most of Change* by William Bridges and Susan Bridges
- *Our Iceberg Is Melting: Changing and Succeeding under Any Conditions* by John P. Kotter, Holger Rathgeber, Peter Mueller, and Spencer Johnson
- *Presence: Human Purpose and the Field of the Future* by Peter Senge, C. Otto Scharmer, Joseph Jaworski, and Betty Sue Flowers
- *Who Killed Change? Solving the Mystery of Leading People through Change* by Ken Blanchard
- *Who Moved My Cheese? An Amazing Way to Deal with Change in Your Work and in Your Life* by Spencer Johnson and Kenneth Blanchard

Suggested Films and Television Series

The following films and television shows highlight the capacity of facilitating change. Some characters may overuse this capacity; others may lack the ability to use it successfully. As you watch any of the following, try and diagnose which characters are overusing or underusing this capacity, and who may be displaying an appropriate balance.

- *Amelia Earhart* (A&E biography)

- *Bill Gates* (A&E biography)
- *The Butler*
- *Cesar Chavez*
- *Eleanor Roosevelt* (A&E biography)
- *Erin Brockovich*
- *The Girl in the Café*
- *The Firm*
- *Howard Zinn: You Can't Be Neutral on a Moving Train*
- *An Inconvenient Truth*
- *Iron Jawed Angels*
- *Jackie Robinson* (A&E biography)
- *Joan of Arc* (A&E biography)
- *Malcolm X*
- *Mandela*
- *Mona Lisa Smile*
- *Moneyball*
- *The New Heroes* (PBS series)
- *Sitting Bull* (A&E biography)

Notable Quotes

If you don't like something, change it. If you can't change it, change your attitude.

    —*Maya Angelou, author*

Leadership is a relationship, founded on trust and confidence. Without trust and confidence, people don't take risks. Without risks, there's no change. Without change, organizations and movements die. Whatever the challenge, all involve a change from the status quo.

    —*James Kouzes and Barry Posner, authors*

By far the biggest mistake people make when trying to change organizations is to plunge ahead without establishing a high enough sense of urgency in fellow managers and employees.

    —*John P. Kotter, author*

Remember, the change you want to see in the world, and in your school, begins with you.

    —*Joseph Clementi, cofounder of the Tyler Clementi Foundation*

People change what they do less because they are given analysis that shifts their thinking than because they are shown a truth that influences their feelings.

    —*John P. Kotter, author*

Activity 20.1: **Roles of Change Agents**

Directions: You will watch a clip from a movie or TV show that includes characters who enact or facilitate change. As you watch the show, identify whom you see playing each of these roles. Note who the character is (by name or descriptors), the situation, and what the character did to demonstrate his or her role as a change agent.

Some movies and TV shows to consider include: *Argo, Lincoln, Friday Night Lights, Glee, Grey's Anatomy, The Help, Hoot, NCIS, The Office, Star Trek, Toy Story, 24, The West Wing*

1. *Change Catalyst:* Be the champion. This is the "idea" person or the one who creates a vision for how things will be different.

2. *Change Implementer:* Make it happen. This is the person who sets goals, creates action plans, and gets the work done.

3. *Change Facilitator:* Mobilize resources. This person helps bring other groups and individuals into the effort as well as figures out how to raise the necessary money or collect the needed equipment or physical items.

Copyright © 2015 John Wiley and Sons, Inc. For use in Workbook only. Not to be reproduced without permission.

Activity 20.2: Levels of Resistance

Directions: Three levels of resistance to change are listed here (Maurer, 2010). Read through each level. Then, identify examples of each level of resistance and list 2–3 strategies to address each level of resistance.

Three Levels of Resistance

Level 1: I don't get it.

This form of resistance results when a lack of information is shared or there is a disagreement over how data is interpreted. This form comes from the rational world of thought and logic. Often, this form of resistance is not consciously acknowledged or recognized.

Personal example(s):

Strategies to address Level 1 resistance:

Copyright © 2015 John Wiley and Sons, Inc. For use in Workbook only. Not to be reproduced without permission.

Level 2: I don't like it.

Resistance at Level 2 comes from an emotional reaction to change. The primary source of resistance at Level 2 is fear—change may result in an outcome that is negative in some way (e.g., loss of status, loss of control). When you are around someone who demonstrates this form of resistance, it is generally obvious, although the person showing the resistance may not connect his or her reaction with resisting change.

Personal example(s):

Strategies to address Level 2 resistance:

Copyright © 2015 John Wiley and Sons, Inc. For use in Workbook only. Not to be reproduced without permission.

Level 3: I don't like you.

When a Level 3 reaction is felt, it demands attention. The resistance comes from an interpersonal dynamic, sometimes even if the idea of change itself is positively received, because you are the one delivering it or initiating it, people resist it. Often times, the issue comes from a lack of trust or confidence in who you are or what you represent.

Personal example(s):

Strategies to address Level 3 resistance:

Reference: Maurer, R. (2010). *Beyond the wall of resistance* (rev. ed.). Austin, TX: Bard Press.

Copyright © 2015 John Wiley and Sons, Inc. For use in Workbook only. Not to be reproduced without permission.

Activity 20.3: **Resistance Can Be Good**

Directions: Resistance isn't always a bad thing. Consider the following prompts to explore the potential upside of resistance.

1. From a leadership perspective, consider how resistance might be relevant and useful. List your ideas here.

2. Next, consider how each level of resistance may be a positive response to change, and record your thoughts below. Refer to the *Levels of Resistance* activity (20.2) for more information about the three levels of resistance.
   Level 1:

   Level 2:

   Level 3:

3. How do you tend to respond to change? Do you demonstrate any of the three forms of resistance? How so?

4. What can you learn from your own reactions to change so that you can become more effective at facilitating change?

Copyright © 2015 John Wiley and Sons, Inc. For use in Workbook only. Not to be reproduced without permission.

Chapter 21   Consciousness of Context

Activities

21.1 What Did You Do?

21.2 What Did I Do When?

Consciousness of Context Defined

Demonstrating emotionally intelligent leadership involves awareness of the setting and situation. Consciousness of context is about paying attention to how environmental factors and internal group dynamics affect the process of leadership.

Online Articles and Resources

- Barbara Kellerman on Bad Leadership: www.youtube.com /watch?v=_nRZWVTrTWM
- Eric Schmidt: Group Dynamics: www.youtube.com/watch?v= wPHL4paHv0o
- Context Based Leadership: http://blogs.hbr.org/2007/07 /contextbased-leadership-1/
- In Leadership, Context Is Everything: www.fastcompany.com /661113/leadership-leadership-context
- Leadership in Context: Transforming the FBI in an Uncertain World: www.youtube.com/watch?v=4JrF2X4Db84

Suggested Books

- *Communication in Small Groups: Theory, Process, and Skills* by John F. Cragan, David W. Wright, and Chris R. KaschBad
- *Creating Effective Groups: The Art of Small Group Communication* by Randy Fujishin
- *The Fifth Discipline: The Art and Practice of the Learning Organization* by Peter Senge
- *Leadership* by Barbara Kellerman
- *Leadership and the New Science: Discovering Order in a Chaotic World* by Margaret Wheatley
- *Leadership and the One Minute Manager: Increasing Effectiveness through Situational Leadership* by Ken Blanchard, Patricia Zigarmi, and Drea Zigarmi
- *Leadership on the Line* by Ronald A. Heifetz and Martin Linsky
- *Presence: Human Purpose and the Field of the Future* by Peter Senge, C. Otto Scharmer, Joseph Jaworski, and Betty Sue Flowers
- *The Practice of Adaptive Leadership: Tools and Tactics for Changing Your Organization and the World* by Ronald A. Heifetz, Marty Linsky, and Alexander Grashow
- *Reading the Room: Group Dynamics for Coaches and Leaders* by David Kantor

Suggested Films and Television Series

The following films and television shows highlight the facet of consciousness of context. Some characters may overuse this facet; others may lack the ability to use it successfully. As you watch any of the following, try and diagnose which characters are overusing or underusing this facet, and who may be displaying an appropriate balance.

- *Cry Freedom*
- *Gandhi*

- *Glory*
- *Iron Jawed Angels*
- *Iron Ladies of Liberia*
- *The Killing Fields*
- *Malcolm X*
- *Mandela*
- *The Matrix* trilogy
- *Milk*
- *Norma Rae*
- *North Country*
- *The Queen*
- *Schindler's List*
- *Sherlock* (BBC series)
- *Silkwood*
- *Thirteen Days*
- *30 Rock* (TV series)
- *To Kill a Mockingbird*
- *Up in the Air*

Notable Quotes

I think it is quite dangerous for an organisation to think they can predict where they are going to need leadership. It needs to be something that people are willing to assume if it feels relevant, given the context of any situation.

> —*Margaret J. Wheatley, author*

Molly Shannon and I used to always talk about that we really felt strongly that we were comedic actors, that we weren't comedians. You just played things real and the comedy came out of the context.

> —*Will Ferrell, actor*

I spent most of my career in business not saying the word "woman." Because if you say the word "woman" in a business context, and often in a political context, the person on the other side of the table thinks you're about to sue them or ask for special treatment, right?

—*Sheryl Sandberg, chief operating office of Facebook*

———————

If you're a baker, making bread, you're a baker. If you make the best bread in the world, you're not an artist, but if you bake the bread in the gallery, you're an artist. So the context makes the difference.

—*Marina Abramovic, performer*

———————

I guess the more serious you play something, if the context is funny, then it will be funny and it doesn't really require you to be necessarily, explicitly humorous, or silly.

—*Jesse Eisenberg, actor*

———————

Sometimes one can be so closely involved with things that the larger context is lost to view.

—*Brian Ferneyhough, composer*

———————

On the rare occasions when U.N. blue helmets have made the news in the past, it has unfortunately too often been in the context of situations where peacekeepers have failed to shield civilians, or even when the peacekeepers themselves have been involved in abuse.

—*Samantha Power, academic, author, and diplomat*

———————

What lists and awards don't measure—and I feel this strongly—is the lasting value of any work of art. They're a snapshot of a moment, and one should always consider their judgments in that context.

—Jennifer Egan, novelist

Activity 21.1: What Did You Do?

! *Note:* This activity accompanies the *Is It a Party?* module in the *Emotionally Intelligent Leadership for Students: Facilitation and Activity Guide.* See your facilitator for additional instructions.

 Directions: After you participate in the two mingling activities, answer the questions that follow.

- How would you describe the difference between the two interactions? How did you feel in each? Which was easier for you to engage in? For what reasons?

- How did you adapt your approach in either setting once you started interacting with others? What gave you the clues to adapt?

- How did you present yourself in the job interview setting? How did you assess whether what you were saying was being well received? What cues were you listening or looking for?

Copyright © 2015 John Wiley and Sons, Inc. For use in Workbook only. Not to be reproduced without permission.

Activity 21.2: **What Did I Do When?**

The setting and situation of every interaction influences our thoughts, decisions, and behaviors. Learning how to read and then adapt to different environments is a key skill of emotionally intelligent leadership.

Directions: Think about two times in your life when you had an opportunity to demonstrate leadership (either formal or informal). Be sure that these experiences are recent enough that you can remember what you did. Then, using the three steps identified below, you will examine leadership in different environments and situations.

Step 1. Label each circle below with one of the examples you identified.

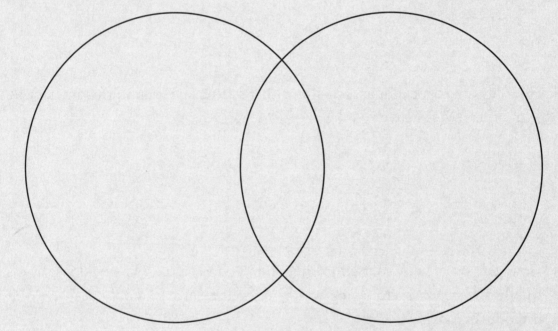

Step 2. Within the circles write examples of what you did in each situation. If you demonstrated a similar behavior in both situations, put these examples in the space where the circles overlap.

Step 3. Outside of the circles write down environmental factors that influenced the situation (e.g., dynamics of the group, time, place, differing goals, makeup of the group).

Copyright © 2015 John Wiley and Sons, Inc. For use in Workbook only. Not to be reproduced without permission.

Chapter 22   Analyzing the Group

Activities

Analyzing the Group Defined

Interpreting group dynamics. Analyzing the group is about recognizing that values, rules, rituals, and internal politics play a role in every group. Emotionally intelligent leaders know how to diagnose, interpret, and address these dynamics.

Using This Capacity

Appropriate use of this capacity changes depending on the setting and situation. However, we developed the following statements to provide a snapshot of what it *may* look like if someone is overusing or underusing this capacity. We then conducted focus groups with student leaders, and they vetted and added to the statements. A number of these statements are presented here.

Individuals who overuse this capacity may be perceived by others as:

- overwhelmed by the complexities and inner workings of the group;

- so engrossed with the internal group dynamics that little action occurs;
- overanalyzing situations when the group needs to move forward.

Individuals who underuse this capacity may be perceived by others as:

- unaware of internal disagreements, internal politics, and other group dynamics;
- unaware of established group norms, values, and unwritten rules guiding the behaviors of members;
- not having the ability to navigate group dynamics in an effective manner;
- unable to recognize the culture of the group;
- blind to situations that can be harming the group;
- unable to influence the group;
- too narrowly focused on something to realize what is going on around them.

Online Articles and Resources

- The Art and Practice of Leadership Development: http:// ksgexecprogram.harvard.edu
- Group Dynamics, Process and Development: www.wilderdom .com
- Group Relations Theory: www.grouprelations.com
- Tavistock Institute: www.tavinstitute.org

Suggested Books

- *Group Dynamics* by Donelson R. Forsyth
- *Hot Groups* by Jean Lipman-Blumen and Harold J. Leavitt
- *In Good Company: How Social Capital Makes Organizations Work* by Don Coehn and Laurence Prusak

- *Leadership Can Be Taught* by Sharon Daloz Parks
- *Leadership on the Line* by Martin Linsky and Ronald A. Heifetz
- *Leadership without Easy Answers* by Ronald A. Heifetz
- *Organizational Culture and Leadership* by Edward Schein
- *Organizational Culture in Action: A Cultural Analysis Workbook* by Gerald Driskill and Angela Laird Brenton

Suggested Films and Television Series

The following films and television shows highlight the capacity of analyzing the group. Some characters may overuse this capacity; others may lack the ability to use it successfully. As you watch any of the following, try and diagnose which characters are overusing or underusing this capacity, and who may be displaying an appropriate balance.

- *Apollo 13*
- *Avatar*
- *The Big Chill*
- *The Breakfast Club*
- *City Slickers*
- *Dances with Wolves*
- *Gettysburg*
- *Glory*
- *The Lord of the Rings* trilogy
- *Lost* (TV series)
- *Miracle*
- *Ocean's 11*
- *Pitch Perfect*
- *Shrek*
- *Star Wars* series
- *Steel Magnolias*
- *Thirteen Days*

Notable Quotes

Synergy is the highest activity of life; it creates new untapped alternatives; it values and exploits the mental, emotional, and psychological differences between people.

—*Stephen R. Covey, author*

_____

There are two kinds of people, those who do the work and those who take the credit. Try to be in the first group; there is less competition there.

—*Indira Gandhi, former prime minister of India*

_____

As you navigate through the rest of your life, be open to collaboration. Other people and other people's ideas are often better than your own. Find a group of people who challenge and inspire you, spend a lot of time with them, and it will change your life.

—*Amy Poehler, comedian, actress*

_____

Organizational cultures are created by leaders, and one of the most decisive functions of leadership may well be the creation, the management, and—if and when that may become necessary—the destruction of culture.

—*Edgar Schein, management scholar*

_____

Culture is an integrated system of learned behavior patterns that are characteristic of the members of any given society. Culture refers to the total way of life for a particular group of people. It includes [what] a group of people thinks, says, does and makes—its customs, language, material artifacts and shared systems of attitudes and feelings.

—*L. Robert Kohls, author*

Activity 22.1: **Layers of the Onion**

Note: This activity accompanies the *Peeling the Onion* module in the *Emotionally Intelligent Leadership for Students: Facilitation and Activity Guide*. See your facilitator for additional instructions.

Name of Group: _____

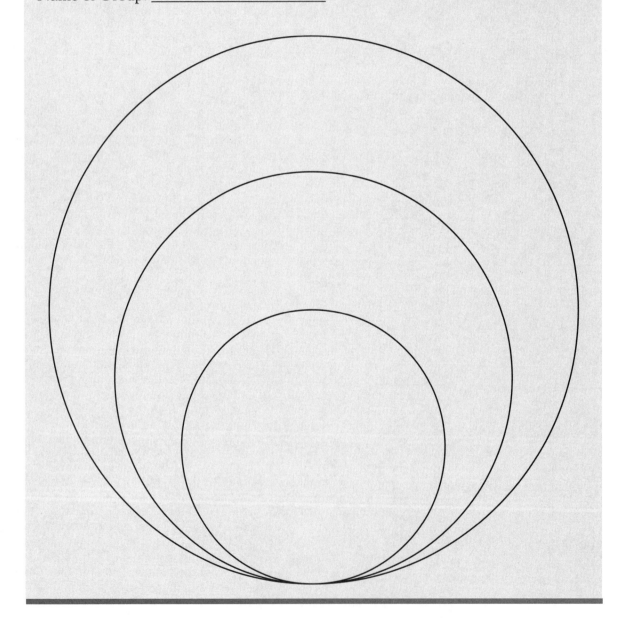

Copyright © 2015 John Wiley and Sons, Inc. For use in Workbook only. Not to be reproduced without permission.

Activity 22.2: **Observing the Elements**

Directions: Below are four different elements of an organization's culture: symbolic, role, interactive, and context. Review each element with your school in mind, then respond to the questions listed and put your responses in the appropriate quadrant of the box at the end of the worksheet. These questions help you identify key elements of your school's culture.

Symbolic Elements = Something of value that all can see or know (e.g., logo, motto, school mascot)

- What do you hear people saying?

- What do you read about the school on the website or in printed publications?

Role Elements = Individuals who by reputation are either heroes or villains

- Who are the people whom everyone admires?

- Whom do people look up to?

Copyright © 2015 John Wiley and Sons, Inc. For use in Workbook only. Not to be reproduced without permission.

Interactive Elements = Shared rituals and accepted behaviors

- What is expected of students at the school?

- What is expected of employees of the school?

- What is typically done by those in each group?

Context Elements = History of the campus

- What is important about where the school is located?

- What has happened in the past that matters to the school?

Copyright © 2015 John Wiley and Sons, Inc. For use in Workbook only. Not to be reproduced without permission.

Symbolic Elements	Interactive Elements
Role Elements	Context Elements

Copyright © 2015 John Wiley and Sons, Inc. For use in Workbook only. Not to be reproduced without permission.

Activity 22.3: Get On the Balcony

Directions: Read the following questions. You will not actually answer the questions provided in the list, but rather consider how they would help you better understand group dynamics using the prompts on the next page.

- Who are the leaders of the meeting? What happens when they speak?
- What do you see as the strengths and weaknesses of the leadership being demonstrated?
- What would make the leader(s) more successful or influential?
- What knowledge, skills, or abilities elevated the leader(s) to this role?
- What do group members do during the meeting?
- How do group members respond to the leader(s)?
- Does anyone seem to have a personal agenda? Is this person supportive of the leader(s)? Why or why not?
- Who speaks a lot? Who speaks but is not heard or given power by the group or the leader(s)?
- Are there subgroups or factions within the group? If so, what is the makeup of these subgroups or factions, and what perspectives or commonalities might they have?
- Who seems to have power within the group (either formal or informal)?

What additional questions would help you analyze group dynamics? List them below.

Copyright © 2015 John Wiley and Sons, Inc. For use in Workbook only. Not to be reproduced without permission.

What Do You Think?

- How might these questions help you if you're leading the group?

- How might these questions help you if you are a member of the group?

Copyright © 2015 John Wiley and Sons, Inc. For use in Workbook only. Not to be reproduced without permission.

Chapter 23   Assessing the Environment

Activity
23.1 Mapping Contexts

Assessing the Environment Defined

Interpreting external forces and trends. Assessing the environment is about recognizing the social, cultural, economic, and political forces that influence leadership. Emotionally intelligent leaders use their awareness of the external environment to lead effectively.

Using This Capacity

Appropriate use of this capacity changes depending on the setting and situation. However, we developed the following statements to provide a snapshot of what it *may* look like if someone is overusing or underusing this capacity. We then conducted focus groups with student leaders, and they vetted and added to the statements. A number of these statements are presented here.

Individuals who overuse this capacity may be perceived by others as:

- spending too much time thinking about the "what ifs";
- being "in the clouds" and unable to make things happen;
- being too theoretical;
- creating false boundaries.

Individuals who underuse this capacity may be perceived by others as:

- making decisions that do not mesh with the broader realities of the context;
- making decisions that do not align with organizational values;
- missing the impact of external forces on the group;
- losing sight of the organization's alignment with its intended purpose;
- unaware of surroundings;
- self-centered.

Online Articles and Resources

- Organizational Culture and Institutional Transformation: www.ericdigests.org
- Strong Culture Can Be a "Double-Edged Sword": http://dayton.bizjournals.com
- What Is Organisational Culture and How Can You Change It?: www.iproconhcm.co.uk/

Suggested Books

- *Embracing Uncertainty: The Essence of Leadership* by Phillip G. Clampitt and Robert J. Dekoch
- *The Fifth Discipline: The Art and Practice of the Learning Organization* by Peter Senge
- *Group Dynamics* by Donelson R. Forsyth
- *How the Mighty Fall and Why Some Companies Never Give Up* by Jim Collins
- *Leadership and the New Science: Discovering Order in a Chaotic World* by Margaret Wheatley
- *Leadership Can Be Taught* by Sharon Daloz Parks
- *Leadership on the Line* by Ronald A. Heifetz and Martin Linsky

- *Leadership without Easy Answers* by Ronald A. Heifetz
- *Organizational Culture and Leadership* by Edgar H. Schein
- *Presence: Human Purpose and the Field of the Future* by Peter Senge, C. Otto Scharmer, Joseph Jaworski, and Betty Sue Flowers
- *Reframing Organizations: Artistry, Choice, and Leadership* by Lee Bolman and Terrence Deal

Suggested Films and Television Series

The following films and television shows highlight the capacity of assessing the environment. Some characters may overuse this capacity; others may lack the ability to use it successfully. As you watch any of the following, try and diagnose which characters are overusing or underusing this capacity, and who may be displaying an appropriate balance.

- *Avatar*
- *Boiler Room*
- *Gandhi*
- *Harry Potter* series
- *The Help*
- *The Hunger Games*
- *Iron Jawed Angels*
- *A League of Their Own*
- *Milk*
- *Norma Rae*
- *North Country*
- *Primary Colors*
- *Remember the Titans*
- *Sherlock* (BBC TV series)
- *Star Trek: Next Generation* (TV series)
- *The Smartest Guys in the Room*
- *Wall Street*

Notable Quotes

I will argue that the term "culture" should be reserved for the deeper level of basic assumptions and beliefs that are shared by members of an organization, that operate unconsciously, and that define in a basic "taken for granted" fashion an organization's view of itself and its environment.

—*Edgar Schein, author*

In order to understand people, we have to understand their way of life and approach. If we wish to convince them, we have to use their language in the narrow sense of the mind. Something that goes even much further than that is not the appeal to logic and reason, but some kind of emotional awareness of the other people.

—*Jawaharlal Nehru, Indian statesman*

Culture hides more than it reveals and strangely enough what it hides, it hides most effectively from its own participants. Years of study have convinced me that the real job is not to understand foreign culture but to understand our own.

—*Edward T. Hall, anthropologist*

The political system loves the extremes, it doesn't so much show a lot of love for the moderates.

—*Claire McCaskill, U.S. senator*

Activity 23.1: Mapping Contexts

Note: This activity accompanies the *Mapping Contexts* module in the *Emotionally Intelligent Leadership for Students: Facilitation and Activity Guide.* See your facilitator for additional instructions.

    Directions: In small groups, discuss the following questions about the maps that were displayed, and jot down key points from the discussion.

- What stuck out to you or surprised you about the maps?

- What other environmental factors would you be interested in seeing depicted on a map?

- Why is considering the larger contextual environment important for leadership?

- What contextual factors are important to consider for leadership at your school or on your campus? Why?

Copyright © 2015 John Wiley and Sons, Inc. For use in Workbook only. Not to be reproduced without permission.

Emotionally Intelligent Leadership

Emotionally intelligent leadership (EIL) promotes an intentional focus on three facets: consciousness of self, consciousness of others, and consciousness of context. Across the three EIL facets are nineteen capacities that equip individuals with the knowledge, skills, perspectives, and attitudes to achieve desired leadership outcomes.

Consciousness of Self

Demonstrating emotionally intelligent leadership involves awareness of your abilities, emotions, and perceptions. Consciousness of self is about prioritizing the inner work of reflection and introspection, and appreciating that self-awareness is a continual and ongoing process.

- *Emotional Self-Perception:* <u>Identifying emotions and their influence on behavior.</u> Emotional self-perception is about describing, naming, and understanding your emotions. Emotionally intelligent leaders are aware of how situations influence emotions and how emotions affect interactions with others.
- *Emotional Self-Control:* <u>Consciously moderating emotion.</u> Emotional self-control means intentionally managing your emotions and understanding how and when to demonstrate them appropriately. Emotionally intelligent leaders take responsibility for regulating their emotions and are not victims of them.

- *Authenticity*: <u>Being transparent and trustworthy</u>. Authenticity is about developing credibility, being transparent, and aligning words with actions. Emotionally intelligent leaders live their values and present themselves and their motives in an open and honest manner.

- *Healthy Self-Esteem*: <u>Having a balanced sense of self</u>. Healthy self-esteem is about balancing confidence in your abilities with humility. Emotionally intelligent leaders are resilient and remain confident when faced with setbacks and challenges.

- *Flexibility*: <u>Being open and adaptive to change</u>. Flexibility is about adapting your approach and style based on changing circumstances. Emotionally intelligent leaders seek input and feedback from others and adjust accordingly.

- *Optimism*: <u>Having a positive outlook</u>. Optimism is about setting a positive tone for the future. Emotionally intelligent leaders use optimism to foster hope and generate energy.

- *Initiative*: <u>Taking action</u>. Initiative means being a self-starter and being motivated to take the first step. Emotionally intelligent leaders are ready to take action, demonstrate interest, and capitalize on opportunities.

- *Achievement*: <u>Striving for excellence</u>. Achievement is about setting high personal standards and getting results. Emotionally intelligent leaders strive to improve and are motivated by an internal drive to succeed.

Consciousness of Others

Demonstrating emotionally intelligent leadership involves awareness of the abilities, emotions, and perceptions of others. Consciousness of others is about intentionally working with and influencing individuals and groups to bring about positive change.

- *Displaying Empathy:* <u>Being emotionally in tune with others</u>. Empathy is about perceiving and addressing the emotions of others. Emotionally intelligent leaders place a high value on the feelings of others and respond to their emotional cues.

- *Inspiring Others:* <u>Energizing individuals and groups</u>. Inspiration occurs when people are excited about a better future. Emotionally intelligent leaders foster feelings of enthusiasm and commitment to organizational mission, vision, and goals.

- *Coaching Others:* <u>Enhancing the skills and abilities of others</u>. Coaching is about helping others enhance their skills, talents, and abilities. Emotionally intelligent leaders know they cannot do everything themselves and create opportunities for others to develop.

- *Capitalizing on Difference:* <u>Benefiting from multiple perspectives</u>. Capitalizing on difference means recognizing that our unique identities, perspectives, and experiences are assets, not barriers. Emotionally intelligent leaders appreciate and use difference as an opportunity to create a broader perspective.

- *Developing Relationships:* <u>Building a network of trusting relationships</u>. Developing relationships means creating meaningful connections. Emotionally intelligent leaders encourage opportunities for relationships to grow and develop.

- *Building Teams:* <u>Working with others to accomplish a shared purpose</u>. Building teams is about effectively communicating, creating a shared purpose, and clarifying roles to get results. Emotionally intelligent leaders foster group cohesion and develop a sense of "we."

- *Demonstrating Citizenship:* <u>Fulfilling responsibilities to the group</u>. Citizenship is about being actively engaged and following through on your commitments. Emotionally intelligent leaders meet their ethical and moral obligations for the benefit of others and the larger purpose.

- *Managing Conflict:* <u>Identifying and resolving conflict.</u> Managing conflict is about working through differences to facilitate the group process. Emotionally intelligent leaders skillfully and confidently address conflicts to find the best solution.
- *Facilitating Change:* <u>Working toward new directions.</u> Facilitating change is about advancing ideas and initiatives through innovation and creativity. Emotionally intelligent leaders seek to improve on the status quo and mobilize others toward a better future.

🛜 Consciousness of Context

Demonstrating emotionally intelligent leadership involves awareness of the setting and situation. Consciousness of context is about paying attention to how environmental factors and internal group dynamics affect the process of leadership.

- *Analyzing the Group:* <u>Interpreting group dynamics.</u> Analyzing the group is about recognizing that values, rules, rituals, and internal politics play a role in every group. Emotionally intelligent leaders know how to diagnose, interpret, and address these dynamics.
- *Assessing the Environment:* <u>Interpreting external forces and trends.</u> Assessing the environment is about recognizing the social, cultural, economic, and political forces that influence leadership. Emotionally intelligent leaders use their awareness of the external environment to lead effectively.

If you enjoyed this book, you may also like these:

**Emotionally Intelligent
Leadership: A Guide for Students,
2nd Edition
by Marcy Levy Shankman,
Scott J. Allen, Paige Haber-Curran**
ISBN: 9781118821787

**Emotionally Intelligent
Leadership for Students: Facilitation
and Activity Guide, 2nd Edition
by Marcy Levy Shankman,
Scott J. Allen, Paige Haber-Curran**
ISBN: 9781118821770

**Emotionally Intelligent Leadership
for Students: Inventory,
2nd Edition
by Marcy Levy Shankman,
Scott J. Allen, Rosanna Miguel**
ISBN: 9781118821664

WILEY

Want to connect?

Like us on Facebook
https://www.facebook.com/JBHigherEd

Follow us on Twitter
https://twitter.com/JBHigherEd